Angelic Heaven
A Fans Guide to Charlie's Angels
by Mike Pingel

Angelic Heaven - A Fan's Guide To Charlie's Angels
Pingel, Michael

Copyright 2006

ALL RIGHTS RESERVED

No part of this book may be used or reproduced, stored in retrieval system, or transmitted in any form or by any means, electronic, mechanical, photocopying, recording or otherwise, without the prior written permission of the author except in the case for brief quotations embodies in critical articles or reviews.

The author have made every reasonable effort to contact all copyright holders. Any errors that may have occurred are inadvertent and anyone, who for any radon , has not been contacted is invited to write to the publishers so that a full acknowledgment may be made in subsequent editions of this work.

Author has either paid licensing fees or have been granted permission for the use of all photos and other materials included in this book.

Library of Congress Cataloging -- in -- Publication Data

Michael Pingel
Angelic Heaven

ISBN 0-9774505-6-2

1. Non-Fiction - Television

2. Non-Fiction - Biography

Published By

Signing Stars Publishing
Henderson, NV 89015
www.singingstars.net

All images used with permission.

Charlie's Angels cover/inside photos ©2006 ABC, Inc. All Rights Reserve. Printed with permission

©1977-78 Hasbro Toys, Inc. All Rights Reserved. Printed with permissions

Charlie's Angels Topps Cards ©Topps, Inc. All Rights Reserved. Printed with permission

Reprinted with permission from TV Guide Magazine Group, Inc.,
©TV Guide, Inc. TV Guide is a trademark of TV Guide Magazine Group, Inc.

Time/People/Who magazine covers used with permissions
©Time/Warner Company. All Right Reserved.

Wella Ads pg 20. Used with permission ©Wella Balsam All Rights Reserved. Printed with permissions

Photo: Kate Jackson pg 141 ©Dennis Kendell Yates. All Rights Reserved. Printed with permission

Photo: Angels in Paradise Scrapbook; 16 images pg 87-91. ©Cynthia A. Lai. All Rights Reserved. Printed with permissions

David Doyle/Kate Jackson pg 78; Kate Jackson pg 190; Jaclyn Smith pg 192
Photos ©Scott Jonson. All Rights Reserved. Printed with permission

Angel Locations pg 186-189; 15 photos; pg 101 Photos ©Joey Marshall. All Rights Reserved. Printed with permission

Emmy Angels pg 41; Cheryl Ladd pg 141; Charlie's Angels Toys (63 photos) pg155-176
Photos ©Mike Pingel. All Rights Reserved. Printed with permission

Backcover Photo of Mike Pingel & Collection; pg 163 (Beauty Set); pg 200;
Photos ©Julie Fick. All Rights Reserved. Printed with permission

Photos: Cover Image; pg 4 (4 images); pg 5 (2 images); pg 12; pg 14; pg 15; pg 16; pg 18; pg 20; pg 22; pg 43; pg 61-66; pg 147
©Farrah Fawcett Personal Collection. All Rights Reserved. Printed with permission

Photos pg 21; pg 42; pg 107-111 (15 photos);
©Cheryl Ladd Personal Collection. All Rights Reserved. Printed with permission

I dedicate this book to the "Sister Angels"
Farrah Fawcett & Cheryl Ladd
without your support, love and friendship
this book would have never happened.

Thank You, ANGELS!
Farrah Fawcett - for being wonderful, always sweet and a rock of wisdom
Cheryl Ladd - for being my favorite angel!
Tanya Roberts - for being so kind every time we meet!

A special thanks to Kate Jackson, Jaclyn Smith, Shelley Hack, David Doyle, John Forsythe, Aaron Spelling and Leonard Goldberg for your work on the series I LOVE!

SPECIAL HEAVENLY THANKS:
Scott Jonson you make me sound smart!!!; Brian Lamberson thanks for being the grammar man; Joey Marshall with your great episode insights; Jules Massey who always keeps my head on straight; Julie Fick for the photos and "What Book?"; Eric T for feeding my Angel addiction; Charlene Tilton you're are an ANGEL in my book!; Craig Nevius for the chase & capture; Chris, Shaun & Ming: my "Haclenda Homeys"; Monica Holmes for being U!; Sean Olson for your friendship; Judith Moose for making me work REALLY hard!; Ellen Louglin for the food!

A Special WARM thank you to my parents Gilbert & Linda Pingel and my sister's family, The McCarty's: Elizabeth, Rob, Jamison & Kendrick, whom I love so much and thank you for ALL your support.

..an ULTRA Special thank you to:
Glynn Rubin, Sally Kirkland, Jay Bernstein, José Eber, Dennis Kendell Yates & Cynthia A. Lai

Angelic Heaven

Once Upon A Time There Were Three Little Girls...

To be honest, I completely missed **CHARLIE'S ANGELS**. And I don't just mean every Wednesday night on **ABC**. I mean, I completely missed the whole phenomenon that was the show. There just wasn't time to experience it. After all, the pilot almost never aired and no one ever expected three female private detectives to beat **KOJAK** and **COLUMBO** in the ratings -- not to mention pull in an audience the size of the Academy Awards or the Super Bowl! But Sabrina, Kelly and Jill did just that. As a result Kate, Jaclyn and I found ourselves in the eye of a pop culture storm that put our images everywhere from magazine covers to bubblegum cards to 3-D mirrors!

But I don't remember any of that: not what night we were on, not what shows we beat in the ratings, not even the fact that we were wrapped in plastic and sold with bubblegum! It's all a blur - as was the release of a certain poster which sold a mind-numbing twelve million copies the same year **CHARLIE'S ANGELS** premiered. What's not a blur, however, are the personal memories I have of "three little girls" from the South who started a life long friendship while pretending to save the world every week on television. The day we were told that our show was number one, I thought: "Isn't that nice?" At the time, I didn't realize the significance of that accomplishment. But what I remember the most is the fun Kate, Jaclyn and I had while chained together (both on and off camera) for "Angels in Chains" and shooting the cover of **TIME** magazine (during our lunch break). I recently saw the outtakes from that photo session and in almost every single shot I am teasing the other two girls and laughing hysterically -- as was usually the case in all our cover shoots.

Just as I'll always be grateful to Kate and Jaclyn for those wonderful personal memories, I am also grateful to Mike Pingel for "remembering" more about that time in my professional life than I could ever hope to. In many ways, I experienced the phenomenon of **CHARLIE'S ANGELS** for the first time through his wonderful collection of facts, photos and fandom. I hope that you will enjoy your experience just as much as you did the first time.

With angel love...
Farrah

A Heavenly Index

Farrah Fawcett's Foreword	Page 4
The Angel History	Page 7
Cheryl Ladd's Foreword	Page 21
Season One	Page 44
Farrah Fawcett's Angels In Chains Scrapbook	Page 61
Season Two	Page 67
Angels in Paradise Scrapbook	Page 87
Season Three	Page 92
The Cheryl Ladd's Scrapbook	Page 107
Season Four	Page 112
Season Five	Page 128
Guest Stars	Page 143
Heavenly Toys	Page 151
Cover Girl Angels	Page 178
Angel Locations	Page 186
Bios	Page 190

The Angel History

Television was a new horizon. It brought people images of the first man on the moon, the shooting of J.F.K., and the hilarious antics of **I Love Lucy**. In the early seventies, television audiences were going to see one the biggest changes; that change was powerhouse producers, Aaron Spelling and Leonard Goldberg.

Aaron Spelling, former actor turned producer, had made a name for himself. His vast career was full of first-rate entertainment, beginning with **Dick Powell's Zane Gray Theater** (1956-62), **Burke's Law** (1963-66), **Honey West** (1965-66), **The Danny Thomas Hour** (1967-68) and **The Mod Squad** (1968-72). The Mod Squad's success started awesome partnerships, teaming Spelling with broadcast giant ABC.

It was Spelling's second partnership that would team him up with former **ABC** Executive Leonard

Goldberg. Goldberg was well known in the entertainment business heading up Screen Gems and was the noted creator of the "movie-of-the-week" over at **ABC**. The twosome became **ABC's** "Dream Team Producers" and together they would shape '70s television.

Spelling/Goldberg began their production venture with television films. Their first series venture was **The Rookies** (1972). The Rookies was based on rookie cops on the streets of Los Angeles. It was a smash hit and the series' stars were George Stanford Brown, Michael Ontkean and a young actress, Kate Jackson. Next up was **Chopper One** (1974), starring Dirk Benedict and Jim McMullan as two helicopter cops in the air; however, the producers second series only flew one very short season.

Spelling/Goldberg's ideas kept coming. Their follow up was a new cop team, **Starsky and Hutch** (1975), set in San Francisco starring Paul Michael Glaser, David Soul and a 1974 Ford Torino. Starsky and Hutch pulled in high ratings and created a second mega hit for the producers.

During this time frame, Spelling/Goldberg had yet another long time idea brewing. "The genesis of **Charlie's Angels** started even before 1974. Television was going through kind of a back alley; a realistic, gritty, down and dirty kind of period with Baretta and shows like that," said shows producer, Leonard Goldberg.

The Alley Cats

"Aaron and I were talking one night, and we always tried to go against the grain, so we thought we should do a show that is very glamorous, very pretty, very romantic. We came up with this high-style idea about three beautiful private-eyes. They were named Alison, Catherine and Lee and we called it 'The Alley Cats.' Get it, "all-lee-cat"?" Goldberg recalled.

The Alley Cats was thought to be an Avengers-Cop type women series. The premise was three women private eyes solving crimes - a blond, a brunette and a red head!

The **ABC** brass, Barry Diller, Vice President of Primetime, and Michael Eisner, Senior Vice President of Primetime programming, were to be pitched **The Alley Cats** over breakfast at the Polo Lounge.

"Not the classiest title ever to come down the pike," they responded, "That's the worst idea we have ever heard. Could we please order breakfast?"

The same morning that the **ABC** executives gave a thumbs down to **The Alley Cats**, they gave a thumbs up to a movie of the week called, **Murder on Flight 502**. **Murder on Flight 502** would star the young actress, Farrah Fawcett. The series **Family** got the green light for a pilot script to be written. Yet, when **Family** was written it was found too good for television and it was shelved.

The Affair

"We did a TV movie, "**The Affair**" with R.J. (Robert) Wagner and the late, Natalie Wood. As part of the arrangement, **ABC** was to put up $25,000 to write a pilot script which would be owned by our production company and R.J. Wagner's production company." remembers Goldberg.

"Eventually I received a notice saying that the time was up, and I called Michael Eisner. I said, 'Look, you're going to have to send us a check for $25,000 and you have nothing to show for it. Why don't you let us write a script? At least you will have a script to show your management.' He said, 'Fine, write anything you want.' So, I told Aaron, 'Why don't we write what we always wanted to write?' and he thought it was a great idea," said Goldberg. They thought right away of their previous idea for **The Alley Cats** and went ahead with writing a pilot.

"I called R.J. Wagner, since he was going to be our partner, and Wagner said, 'I think it's a terrible idea, but I don't know anything about making TV,' remembers Goldberg.

In the offer, Spelling/Goldberg offered Wagner and Wood to be silent producers and receive 45% of the profits of **The Alley Cats**. They gave them their blessing.

For the pilot script, Spelling/Goldberg hired Ernest Tidyman who wrote **The French Connection**. Tidyman finished the original script for **The Alley Cats** and then moved on to other projects. Spelling/Goldberg sent the script to **ABC**. They read it and it was quickly placed on the shelf.

In 1975, Diller left as the network's head of programming and was replaced by Spelling/Goldberg's guardian angel, Fred Silverman. Silverman came from **CBS,** where he had turned the network around as head of programming. Silverman hoped to pull **ABC** out of third place. His overhaul of **ABC** began with rebuilding the current programming schedule. He stumbled upon the original concepts for both **The Alley Cats** and **Family**. He found both ideas very interesting. **The Alley Cats** would grab female viewers and **Family** would pull in the family. Silverman asked the producers if they still wanted to work on their previous series ideas and they agreed to do it.

Finding Angels

Kate Jackson was playing Nurse Jill Danko on the hit Spelling/Goldberg series, **The Rookies**. She signed a development contract with the producers. They thought **The Alley Cats** would be a great star vehicle for Jackson.

To revamp the series concept, the producers invited Jackson's input. During a variety of brainstorming sessions, the rebirth of **The Alley Cats** was coming into focus. While working through ideas, the threesome focused the series on three female detectives. They would work for a "faceless" boss that only contacted them via phone. The series basic premise would be that the three women detectives would get their assignments, solve the case, and end up back at the office to wrap it all up. The women would be independent, solving each case with little-to-no help from their never seen boss. Jackson felt **The Alley Cats** was an unsuitable name for the new series. She spotted a painting of cherubs above Spelling's desk and suggested the name **Harry's Angels**.

The producers found themselves back in Silverman's office with the revamped **Harry's Angels** idea. Silverman swiftly thought of the writing team of Ivan Goff and Ben Roberts would be a match made in heaven as they had created the hit **CBS** series **Maxim**.

The writing team took the ideas of Spelling/Goldberg/Jackson and created a pilot script for **Harry's Angels**. The script hit the producers' desk on October 13, 1975, with a new cast of characters: Sabrina Duncan, Kelly Garrett, Jill Munroe, Scott Woodville, John Bosley, and Harry Townsend. The pilot film was based on three female detectives trying to solve the mystery of a missing wine tycoon. The "Angels" only contact with Harry was by phone and their male partners, Woodville and Bosley, who worked only as helpful men to the Angels but were never to be involved in solving crimes. The next step was casting the leads for **Harry's Angels**.

Sabrina Duncan, was written as the anchor Angel a.k.a. "The Smart One" and was given to Kate Jackson. The second Angel to be cast also came easy for Spelling/Goldberg. They hired actress Farrah Fawcett-Majors who had recently filmed the TV movie, **Murder on Flight 502.** At that time,

she was also known as the wife of **The Six Million Dollar Man**, actor Lee Majors. Fawcett was cast in the role of Jill Munroe, "The Athletic One." The final role to cast was Kelly Garrett. She was written as "The Streetwise Angel" which was much harder to cast. The producers auditioned several actresses for the part. They originally offered the role to Veronica Hamel (**Hill Street Blues**), but she decided to turn down the heavenly role because she was tired of being offered roles due to her looks.

Two other well known actresses auditioned for the lead roles on **Harry's Angels**; Loni Anderson (**WKRP in Cincinnati** and **Partners in Crime**) and Lynda Carter (**Wonder Woman** and **Partners in Crime**). Both were passed over, however they later became ...**Partners In Crime.**

Robert Wagner persuaded Spelling/Goldberg to audition a new young actress he had already worked with on his series, **Switch**, her name was Jaclyn Smith. Smith came in for several auditions. She herself felt she had not done a good enough job, yet the producers fell instantly in love with Smith. Smith came back five times to audition for the producers. "Kate and I took time and rehearsed with Jackie during her final audition for the show," Fawcett remembers, "Kate and I really liked her." The producers finally offered Jaclyn Smith the role of Kelly Garrett.

The roles of the Angels co-stars were to be "non-threatening" male counterparts. The casting of Woodville, the companies lawyer, was given to actor David Ogden Stiers (**M*A*S*H**). David Doyle (**The New Dick Van Dyke Show**) was hired as John Bosely, the office manager. The voice of Harry Townsend would be cast after filming was completed.

Problems with the Pilot

As principle filming of the pilot began in 1975, **ABC** kept a close watch on the progress by viewing the dailies. The producers received a phone call from Michael Eisner a few days after shooting started. He informed Spelling/Goldberg that the network decided actress Jaclyn Smith was not working out. The role of Kelly was to be re-cast and Smith was to be let go. Spelling/Goldberg told **ABC** they were going to keep Smith and the network backed down and gave into the producers' wishes.

Where's Woodville?

In the Charlie's Angels series pilot the character of Scott Woodville, an attorney for the Townsend Agency, was played by David Ogden Stiers. As the pilot was revamped for a weekly TV series, it was decided that only one male character would be needed. So Scott Woodville was axed and his duties were given to John Bosley.

David Ogden Stiers, went on to play Major Charles Emerson Winchester in the hit TV series M*A*S*H.

It soon became apparent that the title **Harry's Angels** was too close to another show on **CBS** called, **Harry O.** Spelling/Goldberg decided to change the name from Harry to Charley's which finally became **Charlie's Angels.**

After filming was finished, the producers' next task was to hire the male voiceover that would be Charlie Townsend. The night they were to begin the looping, the actor they originally hired for Charlie came to the studio intoxicated. Spelling quickly called his old pal, John Forsythe. Forsythe thought it would be fun and came to work in his pajamas to record the voice of Charlie.

Now the **Charlie's Angels** pilot was complete, but once again **ABC** did not buy the concept. Silverman informed Spelling/Goldberg that after viewing the pilot, Fred Pierce, President of **ABC** Television, wanted to know where the girls came from. On the spot, Spelling made up the main opening title, "Once upon a time there were three young ladies who graduated from the police academy and were given outstanding jobs. One is a traffic cop helping kids across the street... one is a girl typing in the office... and one is a meter maid. I took them all away from that. Now they work for me. My name is Charlie." Now the Angels were not only private detectives, but they had graduated from the Police Academy. The new opening gave the series a stern "male" background and Pierce was happy. The producers re-filmed the opening scene for the pilot. It was now ready for viewing tests.

The **Charlie's Angels** pilot viewing test audience was one of the worst ever in **ABC's** history. The network brass now thought their worst fear was true - the show was really a bad idea. They pulled it from the tentative 1976-'77 fall line-up and aired the pilot on March 21, 1976. There were no big promotions and no major stars. The **Charlie's Angels** TV movie took in a surprising 59% audience share. That high of a share usually draws audiences for huge events such as the Super Bowl. **Charlie's Angels** looked like a smash hit!

ABC quickly backtracked and added **Charlie's Angels** to their 1976 fall line-up. The series was slated for Wednesdays at 10:00 pm. The only competition was returning **Blue Night (NBC)** and **The Quest (CBS)**. **The Quest,** starring two young actors Kurt Russell and Tim Matheson, was a new western adventure that critics pegged to be a hit show.

> ### Angel Fact
> *Kate Jackson was originally going to play the role of Kelly Garrett in the pilot film.*

No one would know just how powerful the Angels would be . . . not **ABC,** Spelling/Goldberg, nor the critics. "We thought it was a nice little show, nothing more, and we were totally unprepared for what happened. It was a hit from the start," said Goldberg.

September 25, 1976, Jackson, Fawcett and Smith appeared on their very first magazine cover, **TV Guide**. This would be the first of millions of magazine covers for the Angels. The Angels became the most sought after faces in Hollywood. One lucky company,

"Wella Balsam Shampoo", had nabbed the Angels' smiles and their hair for advertising prior to the series success.

The postman would arrive weekly with 20,000 fan letters for the "Wella Balsam Angels." The tabloids began a love affair with the girls which would never end. On October 17, 1976, The New York Times ran a photo from "Angels in Chains" (episode #4) and ratings went through the roof. **Charlie's Angels** was flying toward mega success.

"I always remember that fondly. When we were first talking to **ABC**, they had seen the pilot and asked about some of the upcoming episodes?," said Goldberg. "Aaron [Spelling] and I talked about the "Angels" getting arrested to infiltrate a woman's prison and eventually escaping. We called the episode "Angels in Chains." When we played that episode, it got huge ratings and a huge amount of publicity. If we didn't stop **ABC**, they would have played it every other week."

From the beginning, the series' success never seemed to stun the actresses and "Angel Mania" was just beginning. The Angels quickly became media dolls. Unmarried, Jackson became known as the "playgirl." She was romantically linked to Warren Betty and Dirk Benedict. Smith became known as the "Southern belle" with her love toward the film **Gone with the Wind**. She recently divorced after a five-year marriage to actor Roger Davis and was now linked romantically to actor Dennis Cole. Fawcett was married to husband, actor Lee Majors, also known as **The Six Million Dollar Man**. She became known as the "Bionic Wife".

-

Basic Angel Script Formula:

1. The crime takes place.
2. Angels arrive at the office to be briefed.
3. Angels are given their covers.
4. Angels change clothing.
5. Angels go out into the field.
6. Angels change outfits.
7. Angels call Charlie/each other for help.
8. Angels change into bathing suits.
9. Angels get into trouble.
10. Angels get out of danger
11. Angels check hair and makeup, while changing outfits.
12. Angels capture the bad guys.
13. Angels change outfits.
14. Angels return to the office to discuss the case.

-

Magazines and tabloids showcased Jackson and Smith weekly, each with different suitors, while Fawcett made headlines regarding her **Charlie's Angels** contract which stipulated that she had to be home every night to cook dinner for her husband. Feminists were feeling that this television show was harming the way women were being viewed. Feminists openly talked about how awful it was to have these ladies work for a faceless boss and use sexuality to get through their day-to-day work. They perceived **Charlie's Angels** as a pimp and his girls.

The actresses strongly disagreed with the feminists of the time. They felt the Angels were strong women expanding the ideals of female strengths. Jackson thought that **Charlie's Angels** was not any more sexist than Rock Hudson was in his television series **McMillan**. In fact, the Angels throughout the series showed that women could do everything a man could do from truck and racecar driving to playing football. **Charlie's Angels** was also the first time three actress dominated a hour of television. They were tops in the ratings!

Even with all the criticism, the audience loved it. Women were tuning in for the clothing and the hair. Men were tuning in for the bikinis. Girls where watching for role models and boys... well...

"People are ready for glamour on TV. Women like watching women. The chemistry between us works," Fawcett said about the hit series.

It was far from heaven on the set of **Charlie's Angels**. An average day on the set would run 10-14 hours. The Angels were picked up in the morning by a limo and taken to their separate $25,000 Pace Arrow trailers where they went over their new script pages and had their hair and makeup done.

Albert Smith

There was another "Angel" on the series that never got his fare share of recognition. He was Albert Smith, Jaclyn Smith's pet poodle.

Albert had his acting debut playing himself in the episode "Consenting Adults." He eventually went on to make three additional appearances in "The Big Tap Out", "Magic Fire" and "Homes, $weet Homes".

Albert Smith played himself in all four.

Consenting Adults - #10 December 8, 1976
The Big Tap Out - #14 January 12, 1977
Magic Fire - #33 November 30, 1977
Homes $weet Homes - #85 January 30, 1980

Spelling-Goldberg's view of the girls was glamour. "Beautiful ladies should be pampered," explained producer-director Rick Husky. "They wore $70 French jeans tailored to their splendid behinds!" Each Angel had her own look. If there was a new style, Smith and Fawcett were wearing it. Jackson found her niche with turtlenecks and pantsuits.

David Doyle had once mentioned that if the Angels had short hair they could save millions! He was right. The cost of styling the Angels' hair alone had been quoted at $40,000 a year (not to mention the two hours a day just getting every heavenly curl into place.)

The budget was now over $2 million a show, which was far over the **ABC** budget of $110,000 per episode. Both Smith and Fawcett were each receiving $5,000 per episode and Jackson received $10,000 per episode. Smith and Fawcett were reportedly receiving an additional $5,000 each for product endorsements.

Angel Time

One afternoon during lunch on the set, the Angels were each wearing red shiny outfits. Their hair was just right and their makeup was perfect. Camera bulbs were flashing. It was **Time** magazine shooting the Angels for their November 22, 1976, cover story on "TV's Super Women." The Angels were hot news!

Charlie's Angels toys hit the stores in the spring of 1977. The Angel merchandise was like **G.I. Joe** for girls! The variety of toys ranged from dolls, hide-a-way houses, radios, vans, paper dolls, walkie-talkies and jewelry items. "Angel Mania" set in.

Everyone wanted a glimpse of the heavenly trio! It even started to take a toll on the production set. Overcrowding began to hold up production of the series. After only 17 episodes, **Charlie's Angels** was tagged a closed set. Friends, family,

Come in Sabrina and Kelly!

Here is an ULTRA rare ad of Farrah Fawcett as Jill Munroe selling walkie-talkies. And now you can stay in constant contact with your fellow Angels with the Pocket-Com for the great value of $49.95!

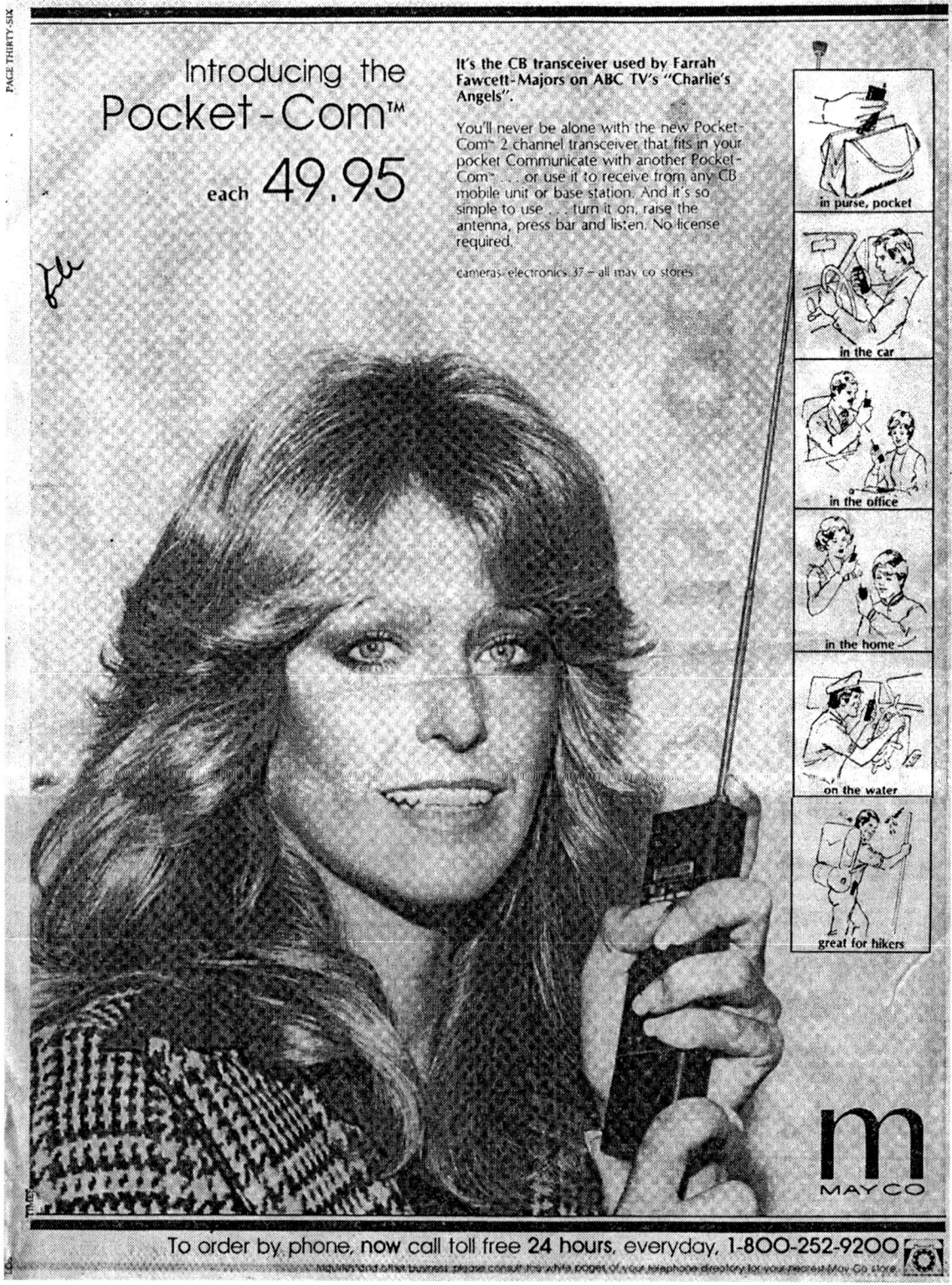

and fellow co-stars had to get permission from the producers to be on the set.

The entertainment industry was taking notice of **Charlie's Angels**. The 1977 **Emmy Awards** announced three nominations for **Charlie's Angels**: Jackson for "Outstanding Lead Actress in a Drama Series," David Doyle for "Outstanding Continuing Performance as a Supporting Actor in a Dramatic Series," and The Mexican Connection (episode #2) for "Outstanding Achievement in Film Sound Editing."

The series was up for "Best TV Series - Drama" in **The 34th Annual Golden Globe Awards** (1977)! Angels, Fawcett and Jackson were competing for "Best Performance by an Actress in TV Series - Drama" that same year; but **Rich Man, Poor Man** won both categories. Although the series did not win at either award ceremonies; **Charlie's Angels** did win "Best New Series" & Farrah Fawcett for "Best Actress" that same year at **The 3rd Annual People's Choice Awards**.

A Fawcett Star

Something else was happening that no one could have predicted. There was a phenomenon brewing. One of **Charlie's Angels** was about to make history. Fawcett had a small red bathing suit poster that was released pre-Angels. Suddenly, it started to sell out. By the end of 1976, over 8 million copies sold of this cheesecake poster. The famous poster was even commissioned to be on the wall in the film **Saturday Night Fever**.

Fawcett became a household name and was seen everywhere. Her face and beautiful mane were showcased on virtually every magazine cover. **New Times** Magazine featured Fawcett on their cover with the simple statement: "In This Issue: Absolutely Nothing about Farrah Fawcett-Majors."

Thousands of boys were calling and sending notes to their all-time favorite Angel and women wanted the "Farrah" hairstyle—the full, fluffy, flip-back style that Fawcett had made famous.

People magazine's December 27, 1976 issue, "The 25 most Intriguing People of 1976," gave more room for Fawcett's photo than Robert Redford, Jimmy Carter and King Kong combined.

17

Angel Logo History!

For the TV series, there were numerous changes with the Angel logo. The most familiar version was used throughout out the series. Showcasing, Kelly with her hands in a karate hold (left), Jill holding a gun (right) and Sabrina with a walkie-talkie (middle).

If a true detective digs a little deeper, you will find that there slightly different logo was used in the March 21, 1976, ad for **TV Guide** (pictured) to promote the pilot episode. This logo had Sabrina Duncan sporting a blunt cut. However, when you watch the pilot episode, they show an entirely different logo featuring a silhouette of the three Angels standing side by side in a "praying hands" pose.

And if you dig even deeper, there was yet another version of the logo that gave Sabrina long flowing hair like her co-workers. This logo was used on some **Charlie's Angels** memorabilia both U.S. and abroad.

Fawcett was huge and about to explode!

Trouble in Heaven

The Angels were unhappy with the scripts they were getting. They wanted to enrich their characters with meatier story lines and create deeper characters. Farrah took her concerns with her character to the producers and was politely told that there is a formula and they would be sticking to it.

Fawcett had another issue of an unsigned contract. When she was given the role, she never finished signing the contract because of three open points including wanting 10% of the **Charlie's Angels** merchandising. Fawcett had one of the hottest selling posters which turned into mugs, pillows and rugs. She quickly learned how much money the merchandise generated.

"From day one, I would tell them I have

never signed my contract. From day one!" Fawcett mentions, "I never understood their lack of concern regarding my open points of my contract."

Farrah announced she was leaving the show.

"I was totally shocked. I heard about it on television. I was home. It came on the news... "Farrah Fawcett is leaving **Charlie's Angels**!" That was my first inkling that she was unhappy. " Goldberg mentioned, "We tried very hard to dissuade her from leaving, but she wanted to leave to have a theatrical career. Aaron and I went to **Columbia Pictures**, got her a fantastic five picture deal. We also agreed to postpone the start of shooting so she could do a film at Paramount [**Foul Play**] with Chevy Chase ."

Fawcett's co-stars, Jackson and Smith, were very supportive and understood Fawcett's decision to leave. That decision caused a rippling effect on everyone. It was even reported that Fawcett was asked to stay for a salary increase from $5,000 to $75,000 per episode. Fawcett said that the money didn't matter; she just wanted out.

The Scent of an Angel

Back in 1978, Farrah Fawcett set up shop with Faberge and produced her own line of toiletries named after herself. The line ran from 1978-1981 and included shampoo, conditioner, hairspray, soap, deodorant, perfume and perm.

Then in the mid 1990s, Farrah once again started another line of beauty items, this time exclusively for Italy. This time around the line included shampoo, conditioner, cream rinse, hairspray, deodorant, and perfume!

As Fawcett finished the first 22 episodes, she found herself in the Los Angeles District Court with a $7 million breach of contract lawsuit by the series producers, Spelling/Goldberg. The lawsuit stated that Fawcett had worked on the series for a full year with the knowledge of the unsigned contract. With her coming to work every day, they believed she was committed to the series.

The court battle started as summer began. Fawcett's co-angels were off doing some of their own projects. Smith was filming **Escape from Bogen County**. Jackson was filming **James at 15**, which she was later nominated for a 1978 **Emmy**. Fawcett also took on other commitments.

The producers got wind that Fawcett now had signed to star in a new film titled, **Foul Play**. They quickly placed a court restriction on Fawcett so she could not accept or do any work until the lawsuit with **Charlie's Angels** was settled. "The whole suit almost sank me," Fawcett said after losing two

Wella Angels!

The Wella Corporation had the foresight of "smelling" success. Before they became Angels, Wella had signed Farrah, Jaclyn and Kate to promote their line of shampoos & conditioners.

And after Cheryl Ladd joined the ranks with Charlie, she was signed to their heavenly roster as well.

An Angel Foreword

As I began this foreword, I smiled to myself because the image that came to mind was my very first day on stage 8 at 20th Century Fox. The show had been on for one season and was a huge hit and I was to replace Farrah Fawcett-Majors. What was the crew thinking? What were they feeling about this new girl joining the family?

I had decided to let them know two things about me from the get go. First I wasn't going to try to be Farrah and second and I had a sense of humor. I arrived on set in a black t-shirt with big white letters that said: FARRAH FAWCETT-MINOR.

Well, it worked. Everyone laughed and welcomed me with open arms. The ice was broken and the day was saved. I continued to find great joy in the four seasons I played Kris Munroe. I would like to give a special thank you to my dear friends Jaclyn Smith, who is as beautiful on the inside as she is on the outside and the wonderful David Doyle. I would also like to thank the crew who worked tirelessly with us everyday. This book could not have been written without them. They were Angels.

These pages uncover everything from the history of **Charlie's Angels**, toys from around the world, episode breakdowns with hysterical tidbits, facts and fashion highlights. There is also a very rare photo scrapbook from my personal collection.

I hope you have as much fun reading this book as I did. I learned some things about the show even I didn't know. Thanks Mike Pingel for your hard work and for you're love of all things Angelic.

Love,
Cheryl Ladd

major film roles.

Fawcett's role in **Foul Play** was given to Goldie Hawn and her role in **Coma** went to Genevieve Bujold. Both films were major hits in 1978.

"If I work from 5:45am to 7p.m., I don't tend to look as good or give my best performance," Fawcett stated about Angels. Long hours and 10% of all **Charlie's Angels** merchandise were two of the three open points that never had been negotiated regarding her contract during that year.

> *"Farrah left after the first year. Everyone thinks she did two or three years. She did only one season."* ~ Leonard Goldberg, Charlie's Angels producer.

As the court battle continued, the producers were facing another crisis. If they could not get Fawcett to return, who would replace her? This could kill their hit series that was riding on a Fawcett-phenomena wave.

With Fawcett's forthcoming departure, there was a rumor buzzing around Hollywood that actress Kim Basinger was the first replacement choice for Fawcett. Basinger had worked on the episode "Angels in Chains" during the first season and became the Townsend Agency's secretary at the end of that episode. The part was never incorporated into the series and the rumor of Basinger receiving her halo never came true. Basinger never would appear on the series again.

Spelling/Goldberg turned their thoughts to a young actress named Cheryl Ladd. The actress was married to actor, David Ladd, the son of legendary, Alan Ladd. Cheryl and David were raising their two-year-old daughter, Jordan. Ladd worked on a 1973 film for Spelling/Goldberg called **Satan's School for Girls** (co-starring Kate Jackson). In 1976, Ladd almost nabbed the role of older sister, Nancy, on the television show **Family.** She lost the role to actress Meredith Baxter-Birney. Ladd had impressed the producers. They felt she had a pure and innocent look that they were searching for in an Angel.

Spelling approached Ladd to come in for a screen test. She originally turned it down. "Aaron knew my work, certainly. I said 'No. You've got plenty of film on me.'" Ladd was also up for a lead in the remake of **The New Laugh-In**.

Spelling continued to pursue Ladd. He bumped into her in a restaurant and asked again about a screen test and she declined once more.

Ladd remembers, "Well, I turned down the role twice. Farrah was all that!"

As the Fawcett lawsuit continued, it was becoming clear that even if the producers did win, their shooting schedule for **Charlie's Angels** would not coincide with the fall line-up. The producers had to do something. Finally, Spelling called Ladd and told her he understood her hesitations about stepping into the shoes of Fawcett.

"Aaron finally got me in his office for a meeting. Together we worked on a character who would become more of a comedic "Angel" and not just a replacement for Farrah," Ladd remembers, "Kris became the underdog who could make mistakes, but end up on top. It was Aaron who thought that my character should be Jill's little sister. Aaron was right; the audience embraced Kris Munroe and took her under their wings!" Ladd accepted.

Instead of a screen test, Ladd started with filming the episode "Circus of Terror" co-starring with Jackson and Smith. The episode was said to be filmed two ways; one with Ladd and one without her so the producers could cut in Fawcett if she came back to the show. During the filming of "Circus of Terror," a limo was sent daily to the Fawcett home to pick her up as the cast and crew waited. Fawcett did not arrive and filming began.

"'Circus of Terror' was my first episode. By the time filming was finished, the whole thing was a done deal. I was the new Angel." Ladd remembers.

The case of Spelling/Goldberg vs. Fawcett came to a close. The final verdict was that Fawcett was released of her original 5 year **Charlie's Angels** contract; but she was to return to film six episodes during the next two seasons. As the case was settled, the producers put all their efforts in their two newest series for **ABC**: **The Love Boat** and **San Pedro Beach Bums**. Both aired during the 1977 line-up. **The Love Boat** sailed into high ratings while the Beach Bums drowned in the ratings even with the **Charlie's Angels** on the show's premiere episode.

The Angel production for the 1977-'78 year was behind schedule. The producers and the network were very happy with Ladd's performance in "Circus of Terror" and sent the new **Charlie's Angels**, Jackson, Smith and Ladd to the sunny islands of Hawaii to film the two hour season opener "Angels in Paradise."

---

heavenly memory

"I remember visions of our wardrobe department, which started out as a very small department. Yet, it rapidly grew to encompass the purchases of our Angels. As hard as they worked, there was always time on Saturday or Sunday to shop and they could shop!"
~Leonard Goldberg

Angelic Automobiles!

The Angels vehicles are remembered just as much as the Angels themselves!

Sabrina had a "practical" orange/red Pinto. Jill cruised around in a "sporty" Mustang Cobra II with blue stripes. And Kelly drove a "classic" tan Mustang with a brown top.

But who ended up with Jill and Sabrina's cars after they left the agency? Kris received the Cobra II from her big sister Jill. Then Tiffany inherited the Pinto from Sabrina, which was eventually passed onto her predecessor Julie Rogers

p.s. The cars were supplied from the **Ford Motor Company**.

Ladd? Ladd Who?

On a large scale the show was on Ladd's shoulders. Stories started to hit the press that the Angels were not getting along on the set. Smith told **TV Guido,** "It takes time to develop relationships. It doesn't happen overnight. I wasn't concerned as to whether Cheryl could handle it. I could tell from the test she was extremely talented in many areas. You wonder if the public will accept her, because they get one thing set in their mind. While in Hawaii, we were thrown together sharing one motor home. We spent a lot of time together and started really working it out."

Would the audience accept Ladd as the new Angel? **ABC** brass changed the show's time slot for the 1977-'78 season to Wednesdays at 9 pm to open the show up to a larger audience. Everyone had their fingers crossed that Ladd could do the impossible and replace America's sweetheart, Farrah Fawcett. Ladd walked into America's living room, on September 14,

1977 Spelling-Goldberg Memo

This is a memo regarding Rona Barrett's recent comments on Good Morning America and how the FBI and LA police are looking into death threats on the Angels.

Spelling-Goldberg Productions

20th Century Fox Studios · Box 900, Beverly Hills, California 90213 · (213) 277-2211

RONA BARRETT'S COMMENTARY ON GOOD MORNING AMERICA
June 21, 1977

The Federal Bureau of Investigation and the Los Angeles Police Department have now confirmed to me that they have launched a major investigation into an alleged kidnap plot believed aimed at two of Charlie's Angels, Jaclyn Smith and Kate Jackson and a third major TV star of another series who prefers his or her name be withheld. The investigation follows this reporter's receipt of a worried letter from a regular Good Morning America viewer...a frequent visitor to California...who didn't know where to turn. On June 8, the viewer wrote that they had visited a Los Angeles Restaurant and actually overheard a small group of people discussing a kidnap attempt of the three stars. Upon our investigation of our viewer's story we then turned the information over to Federal Authorities. We have also learned that all three stars are under constant round-the-clock surveillance and top security with their full knowledge of the case and the possible dangers involved.

1977.

"It could have backfired. People could have said, 'Who do you think you are trying to replace Farrah Fawcett?'" Ladd recalls, "I kept my head down and did my work. I was having fun being Kris Munroe. I figured if I was having fun being her, people would have fun watching her."

The audience did have fun watching her and fell in love with Kris. She did what many thought she could not— she saved **Charlie's Angels** and replaced Farrah Fawcett. The second season sailed easily.

The Angels once again found themselves on magazine covers. Ladd became a household name just after the first few episodes aired.

> ### A Dallas Angel
>
> Before Charlene Tilton took on the role of Lucy Ewing on **Dallas** she was asked to audition for **Charlie's Angels**. "Every beautiful blond in Hollywood auditioned for Farrah's replacement" remembers Tilton. "Aaron Spelling called me in to test, but I was way to young for the role, but I thought 'How can they possibly find somebody to fill the shoes that Farrah left vacant?' But they succeed when they found incredibly talented and stunning, Cheryl Ladd'".

"When the shows finally aired, all of a sudden, everything I did, ate, wore became incredibly interesting when it was not very interesting just weeks before that. That always amazed me. You're exactly the same human being, but now everything is fascinating. I found out fame was a slippery creature."

Ladd's popularity only helped the Nielsen ratings. The series ratings actually moved up and landed in fifth place by the end of her first season.

"When the second season started with Cheryl, we were nervous about the ratings, but they were even higher than the first season." Goldberg mentioned.

At the end of the second season, Angels tied at #4 with **60 Minutes** and **All in the Family**. The Angels were still in heaven. Once again, Jackson was up for a 1978 **Emmy**, "Outstanding Lead Actress in a Drama Series." Unfortunately, Lindsay Wagner won for **The Bionic Woman**.

The series was also up for a second time at the **35th Annual Golden Globe Awards** (1978) for "Best TV Series" and Jackson also shined again as a contender in

Toy Heaven

Most of the merchandise on the Angels came out during 1977 and 1978. Very few items were issued in 1979, 1980 and 1981.

During the fourth season, 1979-1980, with Shelley Hack there was a group poster, iron-on and postcard (and overseas a British Annual).

The final year, 1980-1981, with Tanya Roberts, there was only a postcard. However, ABC did make a promotional poster for the series featuring Tanya. (pictured)

the "Best Performance by an Actress in a TV Series - Drama." The Angels did not win either category.

Ladd had become the sexy little sister of Jill Munroe! As Fawcett did, Ladd released her own line of posters. Each sold over a million copies. Not far behind were her angelic costars, Smith and Jackson, with their own posters. Now the fans could put all their angels on the walls.

In replacing Fawcett, the only unhappy department was **Charlie's Angels** merchandising department. The merchandising producers were unhappy because they had to change most of the packaging. Ladd's image replaced Fawcett's on most of the current merchandise, such as dolls, games, cards and puzzles, and new products such as the fashion tote, adventure van, lunchbox and even a pinball machine were made!

During the 1978 hiatus everyone was off working on new projects. The producers created two new series for **ABC** set to premiere during the 1978-'79 season. First up was **Fantasy Island** and then **Vega$**.

Jackson flew to Martha's Vineyard for a private wedding to actor Andrew Stevens. The couple shared their happy day with close friends. After they returned to Los Angeles they were in negotiations with **ABC** for a new sitcom that would star Jackson. She signed a $6 million deal with **ABC** for three films that were to be produced with her husband. Ladd finished and released her first album for **Capitol Records** which was self titled "Cheryl Ladd." Ladd also began working on a concept for a musical special for **ABC** and the release of her third poster, the "Rita Hayworth pose." For producers Spelling-Goldberg, Smith filmed an **ABC TV** movie, **The Users**, with costar John Forsythe. Even fallen Angel Fawcett nabbed and completed her first theatrical film, **Somebody Killed Her Husband** (originally written for Woody Allen and Diana Keaton), and was then off to film her second movie, **Sunburn**.

Kramer vs Angel

During the summer of 1978, Dustin Hoffman and Kate Jackson announced at a press conference that they would be starring in a new film titled, **Kramer vs Kramer**. Jackson's role in the film was a meaty one and would be a breakout opportunity from her "Angel" mode.

Jackson's original plan was to shoot the series during the week and fly off to New York on the weekends to film the movie. Jackson went to Spelling/Goldberg and asked if

> *Heavenly Memory*
>
> "Sitting on the set and having long conversations with David Doyle. I could never have made it through "Angels" without him. He had a great sense of humor and I miss him." ~ *Cheryl Ladd*

she could work on the film. The producers said flat out no to the proposal due to conflict with the series shooting schedule. Jackson was crushed.

The third season also added Farrah Fawcett's return to the fold with her first three court ordered episodes. "I have approval of the scripts and the directors" Fawcett mentioned to the press about her return. The biggest upset was the price tag she was receiving for her guest star returns. The press had reported that she was to earn $70,000 per episode and that Ladd, Jackson and Smith were all said to have subpoenaed the salary information from Fawcett's contract. The outcome? The actresses discovered that Fawcett was receiving the same ballpark salary as they were, about $15,000-$20,000 per episode.

For fans, Farrah was back! "Everyone thought that hostility and jealousy would surface," Ladd mentioned to **People** magazine in 1978 about Fawcett's return. The first day of filming "Angel Come Home," the set was said to be walking on eggshells. The two stars, Ladd and Fawcett, decided to play a practical joke with their first scene on the cast and crew. The scene was to have Ladd and Fawcett run toward each other and hug. But instead the two stars ran toward each other, missed each other and continued to run the opposite way. The set was filled with laughter and the tension was broke.

IMAGE REPLACEMENT!

WHEN LADD STEPPED ONTO THE SET OF CHARLIE'S ANGELS HER IMAGE ALSO REPLACED FAWCETT ON ALL OF THE ANGEL TOY PRODUCTS. FAWCETT WAS ERASED AND LADD WAS DRAWN IN!

In the third season **CBS** tried to grab a little bit of heaven with two 'rip-off' Angel shows, **Flying High** (which Tanya Roberts screen tested for) and **The American Girls**. **Flying High** (starring Connie Sellecca and Rita Wilson) was about three women flight attendants and their zany adventures. **The American Girls** (starring Priscilla Barnes and Debra Clinger) was also about two female detectives. Neither show could capture **Charlie's Angels** charm and soon closed up shop.

Actress Meryl Streep signed onto Jackson's role in **Kramer vs. Kramer.** The film was released in early 1979 to be eligible for the upcoming **Oscars**. The film became one of

Kris Munroe's
Charles Townsend & Associates
Business Card

Below is an actual business card which Ladd gave out as her character Kris Munroe.

The card has the Townsend name and office phone number.

Call if you need her!

The Strasberg Angel

At **The Actors Studio**, Master thespian Lee Strasberg had a stern rule of no TV acting for his students. Sally Kirkland was a struggling young actress who was working for Aaron Spelling productions to support herself. One day in class she asked Strasberg, "If you don't let me do TV, are you going to pay my bills?" She then made a deal with him and he agreed to watch her on an upcoming episode of **Charlie's Angels** "Caged Angel" (#74).

"The following Friday, Lee shows up at **The Actors Studio,** gets up and makes a speech. 'I just saw Sally Kirkland with Cheryl Ladd on **Charlie's Angels**, and they were magnificent. She was doing feature film acting on episodic TV. I now am changing my rule to will allow all **Actor Studio** students to do TV.''" Kirkland remembers. In 1987, Kirkland went on to win a "Best Actress" **Golden Globe** and received an **Academy Awards** "Best Actress Nomination" for her work in 'Anna.'

1979's most successful films and during **Oscar** voting time it was nominated for six awards including best picture, best actor and best supporting actress. Jackson worst fears came true. The role which she knew was to be her breakout role in dramatic film acting was a success but not for her. Not only was the film a huge hit, but her role now was up for an **Oscar.**

Tabloids reported that Jackson made the series unbearable after the lost role in the **Kramer vs. Kramer** film. It was reported that Jackson held up production, screamed about poorly written scripts and was a nuisance on the set.

Kramer vs. Kramer swept the **52nd Academy Awards** with Meryl Streep winning "Best Supporting Actress" and the film winning 'Best Picture." Jackson and Spelling/Goldberg finally came to an agreement that she was allowed out of her **Charlie's Angels** contract. Unlike her fellow fallen angel Fawcett, Jackson did not have to return to finish out her five year contract. The anchor of **Charlie's Angels** was leaving the show.

On May 15, 1979, **ABC** issued a press release announcing Kate Jackson's departure from the series and a nationwide search would take place for the newest Charlie's Angel. The final episode, titled "Angel Remembered," had the Angels raise their glasses and toast to another great year. This was the last time Jackson was to grace the Townsend Agency.

During 1979, Ladd was ultra busy finishing her second LP, **Dance Forever**, her first **ABC** special, and the **ABC TV** film, **When She was Bad**, which she would receive critical acclaim. Smith wed her boyfriend Dennis Cole. Fawcett was in space with her third theatrical film, **Saturn 3.**

The 1978-'79 season landed at #14 in the Nielsen ratings and once again, Kate Jackson found her halo in the "Best Performance by an Actress in a TV Series - Drama" at the **36th Annual Golden Globe**

Awards (1979). She did not win.

A Model Angel

At Spelling/Goldberg productions the search was on to find the newest Angel. The producers had an idea to turn the Angels into a high fashion glamour plate. They were searching for the right actress for the job. It was like the search for the new Scarlet O'Hara.

Over 150 hopefuls were seen for the new role. The audition parade included actresses Barbara Bach, Kelly Harmon and Michelle Pfeiffer. The producers were being very picky. They wanted the same fire that Ladd gave the series when she arrived.

The two leading actresses for the new Angel role were Connie Sellecca, who was on the failed **CBS** series **Flying High**, and Shelley Hack, who was best known for her hot "Charlie" perfume commercials.

"Connie Sellecca was really in the running for it," recalls Ladd, "I think Jackie was hoping for another blonde. In the end, we didn't have much to say about who the new Angel was going to be."

Shelley Hack had been a model since her early teens and was exploring the world of acting. She had small roles in **Annie Hall** and leads in **Death Car on the Freeway** and **If Ever I See You Again**. Hack didn't even want to audition for the role on Angels, yet her agent persuaded her to fly to Los Angeles to audition. She had to go through both a screen test and a personality test. In a quote from **People** magazine, Hack remembers when they told her she needed to do a personality test her response was, "Oh, dammit. I didn't rehearse my personality this morning."

The Angels were watching over Hack and she was given the newest halo.

Actress Michelle Pfeiffer was beaten out by Shelley Hack; yet Spelling/Goldberg saw stardust in Pfeiffer's eyes and placed her under a development contract. The producers also created and produced a show for Pfeiffer called, **B.A.D. Cats** for **ABC** in 1980, but for the 1979 season they created a new series called **Hart to Hart**. The series was set to star Stefanie Powers and Robert Wagner.

Hack stepped into Jackson's shoes. "We hired her (Hack) 40% from the screen test and 60% from her personality test. We decided she was a nice person with a sparkle and intelligence," Spelling said on giving Hack her wings. Hack was best known as the "Charlie Girl" for Revlon's **Charlie Cologne**. Who could be better to become a **Charlie's Angel**? Hack

Who is Charlie?

It's well known that the distinct voice of Charlie Townsend was none other than actor John Forsythe. Forsythe recorded Charlie's voice in a recording studio away from the Angels.

On the set backsides of unknown actors were filmed as "Charlie". The Audience, like the Angels, never saw Charlie's face.

It's Charlie, Angel . . . Time to Go to Work!

Ever wonder what's involved in filming a single scene of Charlie's Angels? This is a call sheet from June 20, 1977, for a scene to be filmed at "Leilani's" home from "Angels in Paradise".

"CHARLIE'S ANGELS"
"ANGELS IN PARADISE" H-25
Charles Dubin, Director

found in Cheryl Ladd's room 6/25/77

CALL SHEET
7:00/A LEAVE HOTEL
8:00/A SHOOT

Date: THURSDAY
JUNE 16, 1977
5th DAY

Set	Scene Nos.	Cast Nos.	Location
INT/D WAREHOUSE OFFICE	Sc. 12 (3/8)	(12, 13)	4551 Kahala
INT/EXT/D Leilani House & Pool	Sc. 43-46A-46B "A" (1 4/8)	(6, 12, 13)	"
INT/D Leilani Living Room	Sc. 145 (7/8)	(2, 3, 6)	"
INT/D Leilani Living Room (Shambles)	Sc. 114 pt-117 (4/8) (2 v/o)	(6, 12, 13)	"
EXT/D Phone Booth	Sc. 147 pt-147A (4/8)	(2,3)(100)	Kahala Pa
EXT/D Vista Point	Sc. 122B,122C,122D (2 3/8)	(1, 2, 3, 11, 19, 23)	Roundtop

Cast	Character	Makeup	Leave Hotel
1. Kate Jackson	Sabrina	Noon	11:30/A
2. Cheryl Ladd	Kris 10th Ready	8:30	8:00
3. Jaclyn Smith	Kelly 10th Ready	8:30	8:00
4. David Doyle	Bosley	W.N.	
*6. France Nuyen (F)	Leilani	7:30	7:00/A
1X. Dick Ziker	Stunt Coord	(W)	
7. Tom Fujiwana	Billy	Noon	
*11. Cliff Emmich (W)	Duce	12:30/P	Noon
*12. Al Harrington (W)	Ned	7:30/A	7:00/A
*13. Jake Hoopai	Apa	7:30/P	7:00/A
19. Ron Soble (W)	Ace	12:30/P	Noon
23. Art Metrano (W)	Mr. Blue	12:30/P	Noon

X Breakfast Provided

Atmosphere
2 Big Local Thugs   7:30/A Loc. - 4551 Kahala Ave
3 Girls in Bikinis   7:30/A Loc.   4551 Kahala Ave
1 Charlie - makeup at 7:30 Location - Leave Hotel 7:00/A
3 Stand-ins at 7:00/A Leave Hotel
2 Limo Drivers at 4551 Kahala 1:00/P

CREW CALL

Staff	7:00/A	Property	7:00/A
Script Super.	7:00/A	Spec. Effects	7:00/A
Cameraman	7:00/A	Wardrobe (M)	6:30/A
Cam. Operator	7:00/A	Wardrobe (W)	6:30/A
Cam. Assistants	6:30/A	Makeup	6:45/A
Stillman		Hairdressing	6:45/A
Mixer	7:00/A	Crafts Ser.	7:00/A
Sound Crew	7:00/A 6:30A	Scenic	
Grips	7:00/A	Painter	7:30/A
Electricians	7:00/A	First Aid	7:30/A
Gen. Operator		Police	7:30/A
		Set Security	7:30/A

Special Requirements
PROPS - per schedule

TRANSPORTATION -
  THING
  ACE LIMO
  BLUE LIMO

Advance Schedule
6th Day - Friday, June 17, 1977
EXT/D Charlie's Yacht   Sc. 1-3; X2, 10   3/8
EXT/D Bow Outrigger   Sc. 3A-4-A11   3/8
EXT/D Charlie Yacht Deck   Sc. 2, 5, 7, 10   1 1/8
EXT/D Charlie Yacht - Tag Shot

EXT/D Vantage Point   Sc. 163 4/8
EXT/D Wainii High School Sc. 30-309 1 2/8
EXT/D Beach/Surf   Sc. 31-37A 1 1/8

ASSISTANT DIRECTOR Kim Manners   PRODUCTION MANAGER Norm Henry

found herself walking off the pages of magazines and into the Townsend Agency as Tiffany Welles.

"When I got off the plane, there were maybe eight million paparazzi. I looked around for Sophia Loren. It was for me. I couldn't believe it," Hack told **People** magazine about filming her first episode, "Love Boat Angels" in St. Thomas. Hopes were riding high for this new Angel. Director Allen Baron felt that Hack was a bit timid, but felt strong that she would accomplish what Ladd achieved in her first year—huge ratings and the public's adoration.

The problem with the fourth season didn't lie with glamourous dresses, but in the writing of the new Angel. What do we do with this new Angel? The "Smart Angel" Sabrina was gone. Should they make Kris or Kelly smarter? Or, do they have Tiffany take over as the leader of the Angels? Tiffany Welles' background was that she graduated from Boston and her father was friends with Charlie. It would be easier for the audience to accept a Boston girl to replace the "Smart Angel". It seemed simple enough. The writers never could decide on which direction to take Tiffany Welles. There was not much care taken to integrate the new Angel. "My part is minimal because when the scripts were written they had absolutely no idea who the new girl would be," Hack had mentioned about her role.

The tedious hours began to take a toll on both Smith & Ladd. The scripts for that season mainly focused on one Angel at a time allowing the actresses to have more down time from filming the series.

Lack of strong character for Hack did not stop the media event that surrounded the newest

REVLON'S ANGEL

Shelley Hack was known throughout the world as the "Charlie's Girl" way before she became an Angel! Hack was the model for the top selling Revlon "Charlie" Cologne. Her famous walking ad's ran in magazines throughout 70s and 80s worldwide.

Toni's Angels!

Spelling and Goldberg tried to reproduce their Angel success with a male angel spin-off, called Toni's Boys. The pilot was produced as an episode of **Charlie's Angels** during the fourth season. The premise was three men, one athletic, one smart, and one streetwise, who worked for a woman named Antonia "Toni" Blake.

Although the episode is one of the highlights of the season, **ABC** didn't give a green light to turn it into a series.

Charlie's Angel. Hack was landing on hundreds of magazine covers. Unfortunately, the stories quickly turned from "new Angel in town" to "losing ratings." **Charlie's Angels** ratings were dropping. Even the three episodes with Fawcett were not flying high. Fawcett had completed her contracted final episode, "An Angel Trail," and she was never again on the set.

The fire the producers were hoping for with Hack's arrival never came. With ratings getting lower, the producers decided to let their fifth Angel go. Hack learned about her being let go on the evening news after a 14-hour day on the **Charlie's Angels** set. She was crushed, but as a true professional she returned to the set the next day and completed the season. "Shelley was a real trooper and all class. She kept her chin up and did her work." Cheryl Ladd remembers about Hack.

That seasons **Nielsen** ratings came in at #20. David Doyle found his own wings being nominated at the **37th Annual Golden Globe Awards** (1980) as "Best Supporting Actor in a Series, Mini-Series or Motion Picture made for TV. Once again, the Angels were passed over.

Two heartaches happened that year; Smith separated from her husband, Dennis Cole and Ladd also separated from David Ladd.

Ladd released her third album titled "Take a Chance." It was only released in Japan. "Take a Chance," like both her previous albums, would go gold in Japan. Ladd also was in a court battle and won to get her name removed from ads for a porno film called **Taxi Angels**. The ads said, "starring Cheryl Ladd" and in small print "look-a-like". Jackson filmed the movie **Dirty Tricks** and would separate from husband, Andrew Stevens. Hack bounced back with an offer to be on **CBS's Dallas**. Fawcett was offered and filmed a mini-series titled **Murder in Texas** in which she would receive critical acclaim.

An Angel Sings

Cheryl Ladd was known as the only Angel who could sing. She got her start touring around the U.S. with "The Music Box". From there, she became one of the lead singers on the cartoon series "Josie and The Pussycats." And eventually after becoming an Angel, she released two albums in the U.S. and four additional albums in Japan.

Roberts World

During the summer, the producers auditioned 2,000 girls for the new **Charlie's Angels** opening. The producers top choices were actresses Jayne Kennedy and Susie Coelho and a young actress named Tanya Roberts who just had been cast and filmed Spelling/Goldberg **VEGA$** spin-off titled, **Ladies in Blue** (co-starring Michelle Phillips) which never aired.

"I actually did two screen tests," Tanya Roberts remembers, "I tested and they wanted to see my hair a different way and that is when they gave me red hair." Roberts hair at the time was dark brown and the producers wanted her to go lighter.

The casting for the final Angel was a hot secret and nobody knew who it would be. "Aaron Spelling called the house and said 'We'll let you know at 6 o'clock in the morning if you got it and a limo will come pick you up and will take you in and do your make-up." Tanya remembers, "They called me at 6am and a limo came at 7am and that is when the whole insanity started." Roberts won the role of Julie Rogers who was to be a professional model turned detective.

Roberts was hired and delivered to the press and the world as Charlie's newest Angel on July 17, 1980. Her salary was reported to be $12,000 per episode, much less than her Angel co-stars. Roberts told reporters that morning, "This is an unbelievable break for me and I'm going to bust my ass."

Roberts world changed overnight. "Things did suddenly change. That is what happens when you get into a high profile show," Roberts remembers. Fan mail began rolling in and she posed in front of a camera for her very own poster.

Hoping to bring back ratings, Spelling/Goldberg sent the Townsend Agency to Hawaii for the first five shows. The weather in Hawaii allowed the Angels to get back to the daily grind of wearing swimsuits. Spelling/Goldberg had Angels return to their old way - T & A.

"I'll never forget standing next to Jaclyn as Tanya walked out of the swimming pool toward us in a bikini. We looked at each other and our jaws dropped. We said 'Well, now we know who's going to be wearing the bikinis.'" Ladd fondly

TV Prime-Time Line Up

Here are the original TV line-ups for **Charlie's Angels** 1976-1981.

1976 Prime-Time Line Up For Wednesday
	ABC	NBC	CBS
8pm-9pm	Bionic Woman	The Practice	GoodTimes/Ball Four
9pm-10pm	Baretta	NBC Movie of the Week	All in the Family/Alice
10pm-11pm	**Charlie's Angels**	Blue Knight	The Quest

1977 Prime-Time Line Up for Wednesday
	ABC	NBC	CBS
8pm-9pm	Eight is Enough	Chips	The Waltons
9pm-10pm	**Charlie's Angels**	Man from Atlantis	Hawaii Five-O
10pm-11pm	Baretta	Rosetti and Ryan	Barnaby Jones

1978 Prime-Time Line Up for Wednesday
	ABC	NBC	CBS
8pm-9pm	Eight is Enough	Dick Clarks' Live Wednesdays	The Jeffersons/In the Beginning
9pm-10pm	**Charlie's Angels**	NBC Wednesday Movie	CBS Wednesday Movie
10pm-11pm	Vega$	NBC Wednesday Movie	CBS Wednesday Movie

1979 Prime-Time Line Up for Wednesday
	ABC	NBC	CBS
8pm-9pm	Eight is Enough	Real People	Last Resort/Struck by Lightning
9pm-10pm	**Charlie's Angels**	Different Strokes/Hello Larry	CBS Wednesday Movie
10pm-11pm	Vega$	Best of Saturday Night Live	CBS Wednesday Movie

1980 Prime-Time Line Up for Sunday*
	ABC	NBC	CBS
8pm-9pm	**Charlie's Angels**	Chips	Archie Bunker's Place/1 Day at a Time
9pm-10pm	ABC Sunday Movie	The Big Event	Alice/The Jeffersons
10pm-11pm	ABC Sunday Movie	The Big Event	Trapper John, M.D.

1981 Prime-Time Line Up for Saturday
	ABC	NBC	CBS
8pm-9pm	Charlie's Angels	Buck Rogers	WKRP/Tim Conway Show
9pm-10pm	The Love Boat	Secrets of Midland Heights	Feebie and the Bean
10pm-11pm	Fantasy Island	Hill Street Blues	DJ and the Bear

*****Charlie's Angels** ran the final season on Sunday nights from November 1980 to January 1981. The show was moved to Saturday's in January 1981. Then it was pulled from the line up all together in February 1981, and the final episodes returned during the summer and back to Wednesday on **ABC**.

remembered working with Angel, Tanya Roberts.

From the beginning, the final season seemed to be Angel-jinxed. "We had the **SAG** strike, and we stopped working for three months. I did a few shows and then all of a sudden everything was on hold," Roberts remembers. **ABC** also decided to move the show from their original Wednesday time slot to Sunday nights. The Angels were up against mega ratings shows as **Archie Bunker's Place** (**CBS**) and **Chips** (**NBC**).

> ### heavenly memory
> "One funny story, when we were down in Hawaii, they were doing a three shot of us and we all turned around and David Doyle had mooned us. It was priceless."
> - Tanya Roberts

The production cost of the Angels in Hawaii was an expensive endeavor and the Angels were sent back to Los Angeles. It was also reported that this might be Smith's final year on the series. "Everyone knew it was the last year, Cheryl and Jaclyn were not going to work beyond that year, so what was the point," said Roberts.

The Angels were not found as a group on any American magazines. "They did not want another **Charlie's Angels TV Guide** cover," Tanya Roberts remembers. The final Angel group shots were taken late into the production schedule of Angels. The shots never surfaced on US magazine covers, but found fresh life in Europe. The producers had a bigger cloud hanging then a problem the press called "Angelgate."

Angelgate

"Angelgate" was the investigation of producers Spelling/Goldberg defrauding the two other principal co-owners (Wagner-Wood) out of millions of profit. The producers were accused of skimming profits for the sum of $30,000 per episode and a total pegged around $100 million. The investigation did not hit the press until May 1980 when it was released that there was an official investigation by the Los Angeles County District Attorney's office.

It began in October 1979 when the Spelling-Goldberg series **Starsky and Hutch** was canceled. Spelling/Goldberg was diverting money from **Charlie's Angels**, which should be split among all the owners (Spelling, Goldberg, Wood, Wagner). Instead, the money was being diverted as an "exclusivity fee" through **Starsky and Hutch** accounting. When **Starsky and Hutch** was canceled, the money needed to go somewhere. It was put back into the **Charlie's Angels** account as a Spelling/Goldberg "exclusivity fee." Jennifer Martin, a young lawyer working at ABC, found the $30,000 per episode payment and knew that an "exclusivity fee" was unheard of. After Martin inquired, she was told that Spelling/Goldberg had a long-term exclusivity agreement with ABC. She took her questions to ABC's Vice President of Business Affairs, Ronald Sutherland who told her to keep quiet. Martin's work up to that time at ABC was praised, but she found herself quickly fired. "Angelgate" was settled out of court. All parties involved were compensated for loss of revenue.

Letting Angels Fly

Angels season five ratings were sagging, one week the series came in at 59th place out of 65 shows on air. The finale came in at #47 in the **Nielsen** ratings, much worse than the past season. "We're not blaming Tanya for that," Spelling's office was reported to have said.

In January 1981, the Angels were relocated to Saturdays at 8p.m. Ratings remained the same. **ABC** decided to take the show off the air on February 28, 1981. Only 12 shows aired and 16 shows were filmed. Filming of Angels terminated.

Roberts recalls about hearing the news of being officially canceled, "It was right on the set, Aaron came down and brought all the executives and said 'Well this is it' and I just remember being sad - hey that's showbiz."

"Jaclyn & I were ready to move on, we had been through so much together and there had been all the other drama added onto it; Farrah leaving, me coming in, Kate leaving, and there was just a lot." Ladd adds, "Tanya asked, 'would you guys do another year?' and in stereo, Jackie and I were like "NO, love you, but no. We're done. It's been fun."

The four remaining unaired-episodes were shown on **ABC** during the summer of 1981. The final episode, "Let Our Angel Live," was aired on June 24, 1981. **Charlie's Angels** was sent to heaven on July 18, 1981, with the **ABC** official cancellation.

In the end, **Charlie's Angels** filmed 109 episodes including the pilot movie. The show has been seen in over 90 different countries. The actresses of the series went on to their own successes. **Charlie's Angels** was a milestone in television paving the way for women by taking them out of the kitchen and showing them that they too can be as powerful as men. Today, looking back at a series that is over 30 years old, "Sad and a relief. It was like leaving school - a place that was safe and stepping out into the world. It was truly an end of a great chapter of my career." Ladd reflected back

The Stunt Angel

In 1976, heavenly stunt Angel Glynn Rubin went to a huge "stuntwoman" cattle call audition for a new television show with three leading ladies. She was given the most coveted stunt job in Hollywood, becoming Farrah Fawcett's stunt double. Here are two of her high profiled Angel stunts:

Lady Killer (#8)

This was one ultra-intensive stunt Glynn had to do. The scene had Farrah playing tennis and hitting an exploding tennis ball. As Glynn walked on the set she asked, "how were they going to make the ball explode?" They filled it with paraffin, a plastic explosive. While watching Farrah rehearse the scene, Farrah asked Glynn "What are you thinking?". Glynn said "I'm thinking you need a sweater on." Farrah was wearing a sleeveless shirt and the explosion would expel little pieces of hot wax. So sure enough, two minutes later Farrah was back on the set and wearing a sweater. Farrah filmed her part and Glynn jumped. She hit the ball and managed to look away so the hot wax would not hit her on the face, but little flaming bits flew right into her wig and set it on fire! Glynn had the wig off within seconds and no one got hurt!

Consenting Adults (#10)

One of the most infamous stunts was Jill's skateboarding scene. In one of the takes Glynn went round a corner and hit a patch of gravel, which is like hitting cement. In another scene, as her skateboard stops, she is supposed to launch into the side of a car and flip over. However, she hit the side of the car so hard that nobody moved on the set for a five minutes. The stunt coordinator, Dick Ziker walked over and asked "are you alright?", and Glynn said "I don't know yet". It's a miracle was she was not terribly hurt on that stunt.

on the series ending.

Angels Live On

In 1988, Spelling tried to recreate his television masterpiece with **Angels '88** (a.k.a **Angels '89**), but this time around there would be four Angels. **Angels '88** was to star Tea Leoni, Claire Yarlett, Sandra Canning, and Karen Kopins. The basic series idea was four actress who had played detectives on television opens their own real life detective agency; however, the **Fox Angels '88** show wasn't filmed due to script problems. In television history only one show came close to the phenomenal success that **Charlie's Angels** brought to the small screen. That show was **ER**. Even today's critics mention that the phenomena surrounding **ER** is like that which surrounded **Charlie's Angels.**

In 1995, **Charlie's Angels** was the first American show ever to air on Vietnamese television! "Ba Nu Tham Tu" (**Three Woman Detectives**) the complete series ran 6pm every night except the episode titled "The Seance" (#11) due to Vietnams superstitions.

The Angels themselves have reunited in past years. In 1992, Jackson, Smith and Ladd presented Spelling his **34th Annual People's Choice Award.** In 1994, **People** magazine brought Jackson, Smith and Fawcett together to do a photo shoot with Herb Ritts for **People's 20th Anniversary**. In 1998, for the first time, since **Charlie's Angels,** Jackson, Smith and Fawcett were together on film for the **All-Star Party for Aaron Spelling**.

January 1999, **Sony/Columbia Tir-Star Television** released a new show titled **Angeles**. It premiered on the Spanish Network, **Telemundo** on January 25, 1999. **Angeles** was a re-make of **Charlie's Angels** and revamped the original shows scripts for the new Angels. **Angeles** first episode was the remake of "Night of the Strangler" and their second was the classic, "Angels in Chains".

> "It's so special how "Charlie's Angels" is still part of people's lives!"
>
> ~ Cheryl Ladd

The big theatrical movie based on **Charlie's Angels** was on hold at Sony for many years. In 1998, it was huge "press" that the film had been cast and set to star Jenny McCarthy, Jada Pinkett-Smith and Michelle Yeoh. The report was simply not true.

In 1999, rumors were that Drew Barrymore's production company **Flower Films**, was going forward with producing the **Charlie's Angel** film, and this did come true. The original movie script was penned by writers Ed Solomon (Men In Black) and Ryan Rowe. The films story was one of an army of Femmbot Models trying to take over the world and the Angels had to stop them. Needless to say; this version was never produced.

Instead the production team of Leonard Goldberg, Drew Barrymore and Nancy Juvonen hired on a young writer named, John August. August was best known at the time for a hit independent film called "GO." August brought the Angels back to it's honest and angelic source.

Drew took on the role of Dylan Sander and Cameron Diaz was cast as Natalie Cook. The film was laced with problems with over 15 writers re-writing the script to the headache of finding the third Angel. Thandie Newton was announced as the third Angel, yet as soon as she was announced, she was unannounced. Instead, she took the co-staring role in **Miccion Impossible 2**.

The search was on again for the third Angel. Finally, Lucy Liu was cast as Alex Mundy.

Stepping into Bosley's shoes was funny man Bill Murray. The new Angel world was complete as the production cast John Forsythe to return as the voice of Charlie. The film premiered on November 3, 2000, and turned into one of 2000's biggest films grossing over $264 million dollars worldwide.

The "Movie Angels" went in front of the camera again shooting the sequel **Charlie's Angels: Halo.** (later was changed to **Charlie's Angels: Full Throttle**). All three movie Angels returned, Barrymore, Diaz and Liu; however Bernie Mac replaced Bill Murray as Bosley. Demi Moore played a fallen 80s Angel and original Angel Jaclyn Smith retuned as Kelly Garrett for a cameo. The film hit theaters on June 27, 2003, and brought in over $259 million dollars worldwide.

The original **Charlie's Angels**, Kate Jackson, Farrah Fawcett and Jaclyn Smith made a surprise appearance at the 2006 **Emmy Awards.** The Angels where on hand for a special heartfelt tribute to Aaron Spelling. Their moment was the highlight of the evening and made headlines around the world.

All of the actress of **Charlie's Angels** continue to work in the entertainment industry with films, TV shows, guest appearances and the occasional retro show regarding the series which made them household names for the rest of their lives.

The saddest news for the original cast was in February 1997 when David Doyle, the beloved John Bosely, passed on from a heart attack. The anchor of the series was gone. Doyle had told Time magazine (June 8, 1981), when the series had ended, "It was a milestone—there won't be another."

Charlie's Angels Forever.

The final photo of Cast & Crew on the set of Charlie's Angels

The Fawcett

This was the ultra rare pitch ad which was shown to Farrah for "The Fawcett" Necklace.

Episode Guide

Seasons 1-5

Charlie's Angels Pilot Film

Original Airing: ABC March 21, 1976
Encore Airing: ABC September 14, 1976; May 2, 1977

Plot: Vincent LeMaire, a vineyard owner has been missing for seven years and is now considered officially dead. The LeMaire estate is betrothed to his daughter, Janet LeMaire. Janet has not been seen in years. If she does not claim her inherence, the estate will go to Vincent's second wife Rachel. The Angels assignment is to find out if Vincent LeMaire is really dead. Kelly goes undercover as Janet LeMair. Rachel and her lover Beau Creel try to kill Kelly with poisoned warm milk and they find out that the "real" Janet LeMaire is on her way. Kelly is found alive and explains she helped kidnap the real Janet LeMaire, giving her a truth drug to retrieve vital information. Kelly claims that Janet mentioned something was worth $20 million on the LeMaire estate. Kelly blackmails Beau & Rachel for half of everything. Sabrina, playing the "real" Janet, sets up the bait with wanting worthless swamp land for a bird sanctuary. Rachel & Beau buy the swamp land back and then have to retrieve the dead body of Vincent LeMaire from his watery grave. The Angels are captured as they watch Beau retrieve the dead body of Vincent LeMaire. Thanks to Charlie tipping off Aram Kolegian, the Angels escape to safely and the police arrive and send everyone to prison.

Covers:
Sabrina Duncan: Janet LeMaire
Kelly Garrett: Janet LeMaire/Georgette
Jill Munroe: Secretary/Swamp girl
John Bosley: The Bird watcher/Business man
Scott Woodville: Attorney
Charlie: "XO" Oil Corporation

Fashions
Kelly could catch her death in the very small white silk nightgown she wears.

Tidbits:
The character of Scott Woodville was not included in the series.

Star Sighting:
Tommy Lee Jones as Aram Kolegian
Bo Hopkins as Beau Creel
Diana Muldaur as Rachel LeMaire

Director: John Llewelyn Moxey
Writers & Producers: Ivan Goff & Ben Roberts

Season One

Angels:
Sabrina Duncan (Kate Jackson)
Jill Munroe (Farrah Fawcett-Majors)
Kelly Garrett (Jaclyn Smith)

Angel Airing:
ABC Wednesdays 10pm - 11pm

Angel Season Run:
September 22, 1976 - May 4, 1977

Angel Season Rating:
#5 with 25.8

Angel Episode Estimated Cost:
$310,000

Angel Opener:
Once Upon a time...there were three little girls who went to the police academy ...and they were each assigned very hazardous duties...but I took them away from all that and now they work for me...my name is Charlie.

Awards Won:
"Best New Series" for People's Choice Awards - 1977
"Best Actress for a Series" - Farrah Fawcett - People's Choice Awards 1977
Angel Awards:

Emmy Nomination:
Kate Jackson for Outstanding Lead Actress in a Drama Series 1976-77.
David Doyle for Outstanding Continuing performance in a supporting actor in a Drama Series, 1976-77.
"The Mexican Connection" (#2) Jerry Rosenthal, William L. Stevenson, Michael Corrigan episode: For Outstanding Achievement in Film Sound Editing for a Series, 1976-77.

Golden Globes Nomination:
Charlie's Angels - Best TV Series - Drama, 1977
Farrah Fawcett & Kate Jackson for - Best Performance by an Actress in a TV - Drama, 1977

Angel Overview:
America instantly fell head-over-heels in love with these Angels. Was it due to the Angels methods of crimes solving or the lack of bras? No one really seemed to mind either as the Angels worked with their male counterparts to get their job done. These little Angels found heaven on earth in the Neilsen ratings!

#1 HELLRIDE
September 22, 1976

CASE: A female race car driver is killed after she discovers plans are being developed to smuggle stolen diamonds across the Mexican border during an upcoming race.

COVERS:
Sabrina: Race car driver
Kelly: Friend of Jerry Adams
Jill: Daughter of Brother John
Bosley: Brother John

FACTS:
Kelly mentions that she had a wild childhood.
Jill is outstanding at 5 card poker.

FASHIONS:
Jill is very comfortable in her tight halter top clutching the bible close to her bosoms.
One of the few times Sabrina is seen in a low cut dress.

SIMILAR EPISODE:
#46- Antique Angels

TIDBITS:
Kate Jackson performed her own race car stunts in this episode.

STAR SIGHTINGS:
Anne Ramsey as Henry's wife

Writer: Edward J. Lakso, Rick Husky
Director: Richard Lang
Producer: Rick Husky

#2 THE MEXICAN CONNECTION
September 29, 1976

CASE: A charter plane full of heroin crashes in US territory escalating the war between two drug dealers smuggling narcotics across the U.S. border. The Angels go to Mexico to flush out both dealers.

COVERS:
Sabrina: Flight attendant
Kelly: School teacher on holiday
Jill: Swimming instructor

FACTS:
Jill was a ranking swimmer in college.
Sabrina speaks Spanish in this episode.

FASHIONS:
Jill steps out of the shower wearing only a towel to answer the door.
Kelly is caught wearing a new bikini style called "Bottoms Up".

SIMILAR EPISODE:
#83 - One of Our Angels is Missing

TIDBITS:
This is only episode that Jill is ever seen wearing a swimsuit.

Write: Jack V. Fogarty
Director: Allen Baron
Producer: Rick Husky

#3 NIGHT OF THE STRANGLER
October 13, 1976

CASE: Fashion models are being murdered with rag dolls to cash in on a life insurance policy. Kelly finds herself in the thick of things due to her likeness to one of the dead models.

COVERS:
Sabrina: Photo stylist
Kelly: Model
Jill: Model

FACTS:
Kelly is a dead ringer for Dana Cameron, the first model who was killed.
Jill is rumored to be 24 years old and is a huge Roy Rogers fan.

FASHIONS:
Kelly is fetching in a two piece white bikini.

STAR SIGHTING:
Richard Mulligan as Kevin St. Claire

SIMILAR EPISODE:
#67 - Rosemary, for Remembrance

TIDBITS:
Kelly is seen wearing the same bikini in the "Series Pilot" & "The Killing Kind" (#6).
Watch for camera man's reflection in sliding glass door when Michelle is about to be murdered.
Jaclyn Smith dons a wig to portray look-a-like model, Dana Cameron.

Writer: Pat Fielder
Story By: Fiedler, Glen Olson, Rod Baker
Director: Richard Lang
Producer: Rick Husky

Angel Facts:
*Aaron Spelling tried his "Angel" formula for **ABC** by creating carbon copies of the "Angels"! Neither had that spark and never made it into a series format.*

"Wild and Wooly"
(ABC airdate 2/20/78)
Story is set in the wild west, starring three woman who are ex-cons use their wits and skills to stop crime. In the pilot the women try to stop Teddy Roosevelt from being killed. *(guest star: David Doyle) (produced by Aaron Spelling & Leonard Goldberg)*

"Velvet"
(ABC airdate 08/27/84)
"Velvet" had four attractive aerobic dancers as secret agents who use the Velvet International Health Spas as a front for their espionage activities. The series lead star was Shari Belafonte-Harper who later went on to success in Aaron Spelling's hit show **"Hotel."** *(produced by Aaron Spelling & Douglas S. Cramer)*

ANGEL BECOMES PIN-UP DOLL TO NAIL KILLER

An Angel is called in to pose when a slick men's magazine fears it's losing its centerfold girls—to a killer. Starring Kate Jackson, Farrah Fawcett-Majors and Jaclyn Smith.
CHARLIE'S ANGELS
9:00PM ⑥⑨⑪

#4 ANGELS IN CHAINS
October 20, 1976

CASE: A corrupt warden of a women's prison forces inmates into prostitution to pay for prison supplies. The Angels soon find themselves locked behind bars looking for a missing inmate who was supposedly released.

COVERS:
Sabrina: Prisoner
Kelly: Prisoner
Jill: Prisoner

FACTS:
Sabrina can catch a bucket with one hand.
Linda Oliver, a former inmate, is hired as the office receptionist.
Jill is allergic to working in potato fields.

FASHIONS:
The Angels are stripped down and made to shower together.

SIMILAR EPISODE:
#74- Caged Angel

STAR SIGHTING:
Kim Basinger as Linda Oliver
Mary Woronov as Maxine
Lauren Tewes as Christine Hunter

TIDBITS:
The police car chasing the Angels conveniently blows up going down an embankment.
The photo of Elizabeth Hunter that is shown to the Angels just happens to be the same photo that is on her medical file.
Kim Basinger who was given the role as the office receptionist was never used in the series again. Yet, later in 1977, it was rumored that she was the front runner to replace Farrah Fawcett.

Writer: Robert Earl
Director: Phil Bondelli
Producer: Rick Husky

#5-TARGET: ANGELS
(aka Sudden Death)
October 27, 1976

CASE: A professional hit man seems to be hunting down the Angels. Unknowingly, they are being used as bait to bring the real "target" out of hiding....Charlie.

COVERS:
Sabrina: Herself
Kelly: Herself
Jill: Herself

FACTS:
Charlie Townsend's home address is 647 Vinewood Lane.
This is Charlie's first time to get involved with a case in 7 years.
Jill coaches a girls basketball team.
Kelly grew up in an orphanage and she's a gourmet cook.
Sabrina and her ex-husband, Bill Duncan are dating. She's outstanding at chess.

SIMILAR EPISODE:
#79 - Angel Hunt

STAR SIGHTING:
Tom Selleck as Dr. Alan Samuelson
Michael Bell as Bill Duncan

TIDBITS:
The hitman's slide images of the Angels were photo outtakes from previously filmed episodes.
We meet Sabrina's Father.
Charlie's mansion was also used as the location for Antonia Blake's agency in "Toni's Boys" (#91)
The inside of Charlie's mansion was the same set used in the Angels series pilot.

WRITER: David Levinson
Director: Richard Lang
Producer: David Levinson

Angel Fact:

"Angels in Chains" was one of the highest rated episodes during the shows original airing and in repeat. It's the most remembered episode in all of five seasons.

"Angels in Chains" later became known as the "cult classic" episode of Angels.

Angel Employee Card: Kelly Garrett

Born: St. Agues, Texas

Family: Unknown, an orphan -raised by nuns and later raised in foster homes.

Schooling: 1975 - Graduated from the Los Angeles Police Academy.

Lives: Los Angeles - owns three houses in the Los Angeles area as seen in The Seance (#11); Angels Belong in Heaven (#57); Toni Boys (#91)

Works: Townsend Detective Agency, Los Angeles, CA 1976-present

Nickname: Kel

Pets: Albert, a large poodle

Married Status: Single

Best Friends: Jill Munroe, Sabrina Duncan, Kris Munroe, Tiffany Welles, Julie Rogers, John Bosley — associates at the Townsend Agency; Sally Miles — best friend for years, met at summer camp (#57); Sharon — old friends from High School (#72) Lilibet - her childhood doll (#11)

Car: Ford Mustang - Tan — company car

Boyfriends: Dr. Alan Samuelson (#5), Ted Machlin (#44); Bill Freedman (#49); Bill Cord (#92 & #93)

Interests: Cooking, fine wines, the gun range, good bathing suits and donates her time working with autistic children.

Best Detective Skills: Picking Locks and Shooting

#6 -- THE KILLING KIND
November 3, 1976

CASE: A writer is murdered after she writes an in-depth expose about the owner of a luxurious resort and his shady dealings.

COVERS:
Sabrina: Fashion designer
Kelly: Photographer and writer for "Fashion Daily"
Jill: Tennis instructor
Bosley: Model

FACTS:
We find out in this episode that Charlie has an ex-wife and Bosley is married.
Jill samples "Sunday's Undies."

FASHIONS:
Kelly and Jill are found in terri cloth towels getting a massage by Inga.
Kelly is found once again in her trademark white bikini, also seen in the pilot film & "Night of the Strangler" (#3).

STAR SIGHTING:
Robert Loggia as Paul Terranova

TIDBITS:
The vehicle that Sabrina runs off the road blows up in mid-air before crashing.
While Kelly is in Terranova's office, her hair is messy as she swings her hair around. As the camera captures a close-up, her hair is miraculously styled.
The resort used as the backdrop for this episode is also used in two other angel episodes, "Angels on a String" (#15) & "Angel in a Box" (#63).

WRITER: Rick Husky
DIRECTOR: Richard Benedict
Producer: Rick Husky

#7—TO KILL AN ANGEL
November 10, 1976

CASE: Kelly and an orphaned boy are visiting an amusement park while a killing is taking place. The orphaned boy stumbles across the gun and accidentally shoots Kelly in the head.

COVERS:
Sabrina: Herself
Kelly: Gunshot victim
Jill: Herself

FACTS:
Kelly does volunteer work in her spare time.

SIMILAR EPISODE:
#109 - Let Our Angel Live

TIDBITS:
A character in this episode is spotted wearing a "Starsky & Hutch" T-shirt. A little Spelling/Goldberg show plug!
Kelly was also shot in the head in the episode "Let Our Angel Live" (#109)

WRITER: Rick Husky
DIRECTOR: Phil Bondelli
Producers: Aaron Spelling & Leonard Goldberg

"Pretty Is As Pretty Does"
This is one of Kelly's most famous lines.
She uses it in two episodes:
Angels Remembered (#68)
& Love Boat Angels (#69)

CHARLIE'S ANGELS
Special Double Feature!

Tonight, enjoy two of the Angel's most exciting adventures—two cases of mysterious murder! Kate Jackson, Farrah Fawcett-Majors, Jaclyn Smith star.
CHARLIE'S ANGELS
9:00-11:00PM

#8-LADY KILLER
November 24, 1976

CASE: Beautiful female centerfolds from "Feline Magazine" are being targeted by a serial killer. Jill goes undercover as a Feline centerfold and finds herself the next target.

COVERS:
Sabrina: Tony's girlfriend
Kelly: Club singer
Jill: Centerfold

FASHIONS:
Jill is found prancing around in a feline outfit when she's not slipping into a silk nightgown. Sweet dreams!

TIDBITS:
Jaclyn Smith is seen wearing the pink Nolan Miller gown that she made famous when she wore it on the November 22, 1976, **Time** magazine cover.
Jill Munroe's "Feline" outfit is the same costume that her sister Kris Munroe wears on "Circus of Terror" (# 27).
This episode was loosely based on Hugh Hefner and his **Playboy** club.

Writer: Sue Milburn
Director: George McCowan
Producer: David Levinson

SPECIAL! 90-MINUTE MOVIE!
The Angels dig into the disappearance of a wealthy winegrower... and run into a deadly bottleneck. Starring Kate Jackson, Farrah Fawcett-Majors, Jaclyn Smith.
CHARLIE'S ANGELS
abc **7:00PM** ⑨

ANGELS SMOKE OUT VICIOUS CRIMINAL AFTER "ADULT" FILM STUDIO FIRE!
A fire exposes a clue that puts the Angels on a surprising trail of crime and intrigue. Kate Jackson, Farrah Fawcett-Majors, Jaclyn Smith star.
CHARLIE'S ANGELS
abc **9:00PM** ⑰ ⑲ ㊳

Angel Fact

Famous Hairstylist José Eber set off a world-wide hair craze when he created with Fawcett the infamous "Farrah" hairdo in the '70s!

#9 - BULLSEYE
December 1, 1976

CASE: A female army recruit is murdered. The Angels enlist in the Army and expose an illegal drug operation.

COVERS:
Sabrina: Nurse
Kelly: Army recruit
Jill: Army recruit
Bosley: Researcher

FACTS:
Sabrina's father was a General in the Army.

FASHIONS:
The girls look great in fatigues. The way their clothes fit, one wonders what designer the Army uses. Gives "Be All You Can Be" a new meaning!

TIDBIT:
While filming "Bullseye" two angels, Kate Jackson & Jaclyn Smith celebrated their birthdays on the set.

STAR SIGHTINGS:
Robert Pine as Dr. Conlan

WRITER: Jeff Myrow
DIRECTOR: Daniel Haller
PRODUCER: David Levinson

#10 - CONSENTING ADULTS
December 8, 1976

CASE: An antique store owner has been robbed and kidnapped after becoming involved with the "Consenting Adults" dating service.

COVERS:
Sabrina: Kidnapped
Kelly: Editor for "New Sport" magazine
Jill: Prostitute
Bosley: Client at "Consenting Adults"

FACTS:
Kelly loves her tequila straight up with salt & lime.
This episode holds Jill's famous skateboard get-a-way scene.

SIMILAR EPISODE:
45 - Angels on the Run

STAR SIGHTING:
Laurette Spang as Tracy Martel

TIDBITS:
While in their cars, why were the Angels talking via walkie-talkies instead of their car phones? Did Bosley forget to make that month's payment?
Albert Smith, Jaclyn's dog makes his first appearance.

Writer: Les Carter
Director: George McCowan
Producer: David Levinson

Angel Hair

Charlie's Angels became famous overnight not only for their beauty, but also for their hair style! Here is an ad from 1977 which displays "The Angel Collection."

Blow-dryers went flying after this was spotted! The Angels wigs were never officially licenced.

Angel Employee Card: Jill Munroe

Born: Los Angeles, CA

Family: Sister Kris Munroe, Aunt & Uncle (#59), an alcoholic father (#87),

Schooling: 1975 - graduated from the Los Angeles Police Academy

Address: 2734 Ocean Way, Malibu, CA

Phone: (213) 555-1472

Employment:
Townsend Detective Agency, Los Angeles 1976-1977

Current: Race Car Driver 1977-present

Awards: Won the Grand Prix 1977.

Nickname: None

Pets: None

Boyfriends: Jericho (#13); Damien Roth (#73) Prince Eric (#76)

Marriage: Never married but was engaged to Steve Carmody (#48)

Best Friends: Kelly Garrett, Sabrina Duncan, John Bosley —associates at the Townsend Agency

Car: Ford Cobra - white with Blue Strip — company car

Interests: Dancing, racing cars, sports enthusiast, basketball coach, hair and teeth products.

Best Detective Skills: Sexuality and lots of hair.

#11 - THE SEANCE
(aka Medium Cool)
December 15, 1976

CASE: A wealthy woman is conned out of her priceless jewelry by a hypnotist.

COVERS:
Sabrina: Secretary
Kelly: Rich oil heiress
Jill: Assistant to Kelly
Bosley: Chauffeur

FACTS:
Kelly was abused as a child and has a rag doll named "Lilibet."

FASHIONS:
Kelly walks the streets of Los Angeles in a trance in her sexy white silk night gown. A truly hot city!

SIMILAR EPISODE
#106 - Attack Angels

TIDBITS:
In a later episode "Angels in Springtime" (#50), Kelly refers to this episode to be the reason she cannot be hypnotized.

STAR SIGHTING:
Rene Auberjonois as Terrance
Carole Cook as Madame Dorian
Gertude Flynn as Grace Rodeheaver

WRITER: Roberts Dennis
DIRECTOR: George Brooke
PRODUCER: Barney Rosenweig

> **Angel Fact:**
> Farrah Fawcett's famous red swimsuit poster sold over 12 million copies!

#12 - ANGELS ON WHEELS
(aka DEATH ON WHEELS)
December 22, 1976

CASE: A roller derby skater is murdered while participating in an insurance scam.

COVERS:
Sabrina: Investigator for California State Board of Insurance
Kelly: "Woman's View" magazine reporter
Jill: "Barbara Jason" roller derby skater; sister of murdered girl

FACTS:
Kelly's license plate number is CA 356CFX.
Sabrina is found drinking a Diet Dr. Pepper.

STAR SIGHTING:
Dick Sargent as Hugh Morris

TIDBITS:
During stunt driving sequence when Kelly's car screeches to a halt, background cars disappear. An older Mustang was used in the explosion of Kelly's car. Then after her car was blown up, we see Kelly's Mustang parked in front of the office!
This is one of the few episodes we see the Angels eating while discussing a case.
How does Charlie know there is a bomb attached to Kelly's car???

WRITER: Charles Sailor, Jack V. Fogarty and Rick Husky
DIRECTOR: Richard Benedict
PRODUCER: Rick Husky

#13 - ANGEL TRAP
(aka: Where Do Warriors Weep? & Jericho)
January 5, 1977

CASE: A hit man is hired to assassinate the remaining survivors of an old time Army Intelligence Unit. Jill befriends the assassin to stop his next killing.

COVERS:
Sabrina: Girlfriend to John Kamden
Kelly: Hot dog vendor
Jill: Model from Portland, Oregon
Bosley: Mr. Johnson

FACTS:
Jill's phone number is 555-1472.

FASHIONS:
Kelly is seen running into Jill's home with a two piece black bathing suit and silk robe. She could catch her death!

STAR SIGHTING:
Fernando Lamas as Jericho

TIDBITS:
In the capture scene, watch closely as Sabrina's clothes change. At a distance, she's wearing a tan and brown outfit, in her close-up, the outfit miraculously turns red. Then as she's shown at a distance again, it turns back to tan and brown.
We see Jill's business card with her home address and phone number.

WRITER: Edward J. Lakso
DIRECTOR: Georg McCowan
PRODUCER: Barney Rosenzweig

#14 - THE BIG TAP OUT
January 12, 1977

CASE: The Angels out con a con man at his own game.

COVERS:
Sabrina: Gambler
Kelly: Kelly Duncan - sister to Sabrina
Jill: Cindy Peepers
Bosley: Chip the bookie; Jim Joe Peepers

SIMILAR EPISODE
#90 Three For the Money

TIDBITS
Albert Smith, Jaclyn's poodle makes his second guest appearance.

WRITER: Brian McKay
DIRECTOR: Georg Stanford Brown
PRODUCER: Barney Rosenzweig

#15 - ANGELS ON A STRING
(aka: Fast Dance on a Slow Mountain)
January 19, 1977

CASE: The Angels take a vacation together and stumble across the kidnapping of a Polish political writer.

COVERS:
Sabrina: Waitress
Kelly: Herself
Jill: Maid

FACTS:
Sabrina has a "huge" crush on Peter Wycinski and eventually agrees to go out on a date with his son.

SIMILAR EPISODE:
#59 Angels on Vacation

FASHIONS:
It's the middle of winter, Kelly is modeling her new bikini by the pool while Sabrina is still wrapped up in sweater.

TIDBITS:
Isn't it amazing how a towel draped on a hanger in a shower can resemble Sabrina.
The resort was also used in "The Killing Kind" (#6) and "Angel in the Box" (#63).

WRITER: Edward J. Lakso
DIRECTOR: Larry Doheny
PRODUCER: Barney Rosenqweig

#16 DIRTY BUSINESS
February 2, 1977

CASE: A blackmailing pornographer is being terrorized by a crooked District Attorney.

COVERS:
Sabrina: Reporter for "Earth Gazette" newspaper
Kelly: Wannabe porno star
Jill: Herself

FACTS:
Charlie has a fish called "Millicent" who is sick.
Jill's license plate # CA 861BMG and she also happens to have the key to Sabrina's parking garage.

TIDBITS:
The original air date of this episode aired on Farrah Fawcett's birthday.

WRITER: Edward J. Lakso
DIRECTOR: Bill Bixby
PRODUCER: Barney Rosenweig

#17 THE VEGAS CONNECTION
February 9, 1977

CASE: A crooked casino manager photographs his hotel guests and employees in their indiscreational activities and then blackmails them.

COVERS:
Sabrina: Insurance representative/state auditor
Kelly: Showgirl
Jill: Horoolf
Bosley: Vegas high roller Will Thurman

FASHIONS:
Kelly is seen dancing around in a leotard.

TIDBITS:
Bosley gets his first big kiss (hope Mrs. Bosley doesn't find out). Mentioned in "The Killing Kind" (#6), that Bosley is married.

WRITER: John D.F. Black
DIRECTOR: Georg McCowan
PRODUCER: Barney Rosenweig

Brie: Held Hostage

Consenting Adults (#10) Sabrina is tied-up & blind folded while gunshots are fired around her head.
Pretty Angels All in a Row (#25) Sabrina is tied-up and held for ransom.
Angels on the Air (#30) Sabrina is tied-up and given a truth drug.
Magic Fire (#33) Sabrina is tied-up & gagged in a burning building.
Terror on Skis (#62): Sabrina is held hostage in a ski cabin.

Premiere Tonight! Jaclyn Smith, Farrah Fawcett-Majors and Kate Jackson star as three beautiful private eyes who are up to their eyes in murder, danger and crime. From the producers of Starsky & Hutch.

CHARLIE'S ANGELS
ABC 10:00PM ⑨ ⑩ ㊵

Brie's Husband

Actor, Michael Bell played Bill Duncan the ex-husband of the "Smart" Angel Sabrina Duncan. Bill Duncan was seen in two episodes "Target: Angels" (#5) and "The Blue Angels" (#22). His character was dropped from the storyline with the cutting down of the Angels outside life from the Agency work.

Michael Bell went on to play roles on these hit series: **Dallas, Star Trek** and **Rugrats**.

First Season Opening Sequence (1976-1977)

1. Police Academy Shot
2. Sabrina at police Firing Range
3. Jill on police survivor course
4. Kelly in police defense class
5. Sabrina an police parking attendant
6. Jill doing police paper work
7. Kelly a police crosswalk guard
8. All three Angels walking out of Police Department
9. Silhouette Angel with Walkie-Talkie and lettering "Kate Jackson"
10. Sabrian Race Car Driver - Episode "Hellride"
11. Sabrina Turns to camera - "The Killing Kind"
12. Sabrina Running - Episode "Pilot Film"
13. Sabrina Squatting - Episode "Pilot Film"
14. Sabrina Aiming Gun - episode "The Killing Kind"
15. Silhouette Angel with Gun and lettering "Farrah Fawcett-Majors"
16. Jill on roller skates - Episode "Angels on Wheels"
17. Jill in Black - Episode "The Killing Kind"
18. Jill in a towel - Episode "The Killing Kind"
19. Jill is driving - Episode "Hellride"
20. Jill playing Tennis - Episode "Pilot Film"
21. Silhouette Angel Karate Chopping and lettering "Jaclyn Smith"
22. Kelly running from her car - Episode "Angels on Wheels"
23. Kelly on motor cycle - Episode "Pilot Film"
24. Kelly taking a photo with camera - Episode "The Killing Kind"
25. Kelly doing a turn and putting on a hat - Episode "Night of the Strangler"
26. Kelly with head over shoulder - Episode "The Killing Kind"
27. Silhouette of Bosley and lettering "David Doyle"
28. Bosley hugging Sabrina - Episode "Hellride"
29. Bosley handing a gift - Episode "Hellride"
30. Charlie's Angels Logo and Exploding

Lovestories

Season One

The Mexican Connection
(episode #2)
Sabrina fell for Jim Taylor while undercover; however Jim was a drug dealer and a killer.

Target Angels
(episode #5)
Kelly Garrett is found dating Dr. Alan Samuelson (Tom Selleck) yet feels she needs to break it off after she is a target of a killer. The good Doctor is never to been seen again.

Lady Killer
(episode #8)
Sabrina has a crush on the Angels client, Tony Mann, the owner of "Feline" magazine. Mann only has eyes for his centerfolds!

Angel Trap
(episode #13)
Jill Munroe uses her charm to get close to a professional hitman known as "Jericho". Jill falls for him while he is in a process of a hit.

Angel on a String
(episode #15)
Sabrina finds feelings for her Russian idol, Peter Wychinski. Her lust for Wychinskis' smarts sends the Angels searching for his kidnappers. In the end, Wychinski is too old for Sabrina, but she might be the right age to date his son.

Angel Facts!
Here are the angelic ages of each Angel when they joined the agency!

**Fawcett: 29   Smith: 29   Jackson: 27
Ladd: 26   Hack: 30   Roberts: 26**

#18 - TERROR ON WARD ONE
February 16, 1977

CASE: Nurses at a local hospital are being terrorized by a mad man.

COVERS:
Sabrina: Reporter for "Medical Journal"
Kelly: Student nurse
Jill: Student nurse
Bosley: Patient

FACTS:
Bosley checks into the hospital for an ingrown toe nail. After his medial records are switched, he ends up with having his appendix removed.

FASHIONS:
Jill looks fine in her nurses uniform as she uses her feminine way to interrogate Quincy. the kissing intern

WRITER: Edward J. Lakso
DIRECTOR: Bob Kelljan
PRODUCER: Barney Rosenzweig

#19 - DANCING IN THE DARK
February 23, 1977

CASE: A widow is being blackmailed with photographs of her in a compromising position.

COVERS:
Sabrina: Sabrina Walker, a rich woman
Kelly: Sleazy private detective
Jill: Dance instructor
Bosley: The impostor Mr. Walker
Charlie: The real Mr. Walker

FACTS:
Jill as a dancing instructor shows that she is an excellent disco dancer.
Charlie actually has a role in this episode as he plays the chauffeur to Bosley, and the "real" Mr. Walker

FASHIONS:
Jill is dancing her little heart out wearing a low cut vest.

STAR SIGHTING:
Dennis Cole as Tony Bordinay

WRITER: Les Carter
DIRECTOR: Cliff Bole
PRODUCER: Barney Rosenweig

#20 - I WILL BE REMEMBERED
March 9, 1977

CASE: A fading film star is terrorized when she attempts a comeback.

COVERS:
Sabrina: Secretary
Kelly: Film extra
Jill: Press reporter

FACTS:
Sabrina can't cook.
Gloria Gibson is an old friend of Charlie's.

FASHIONS:
Sabrina walking around in a silk robe.

STAR SIGHTING:
Ida Lupino as Gloria Gibson

TIDBITS:
This was Ida Lupino's last television performance. Lupino's husband, Howard Duff appears in "Harrigan's Angels" (#87).

WRITER: Melvin Levy
DIRECTOR: Nicholas Sgarro
PRODUCER: Barney Rosenzweig

#21—ANGEL AT SEA
(aka: The Shortest Voyage Home)
March 23, 1977

CASE: A cruise line is on the brink of bankruptcy due to a string of accidents.

COVERS:
Sabrina: Herself
Kelly: Fakes her death
Jill: Herself

FACTS:
This is the only time Bosley is seen semi-nude!
Sabrina looses her "new" bikini in her cabin fire.

FASHIONS:
The Angels are found running around the ship in their pajamas trying to catch that crazy bad guy! "Man over board!"

TIDBITS:
Portions of this episode were shot on location aboard **The Queen Mary** in Long Beach, California.

STAR SIGHTING:
Frank Gorshin as Harry Dana

WRITER: John D.F. Black
DIRECTOR: Allen Baron
PRODUCER: Barney Rosenzweig

#22 - THE BLUE ANGELS
May 4, 1977

CASE: A murder at a massage parlor leads to corruption with in the Los Angeles police department.

COVERS:
Sabrina: On assignment from the Phoenix police department
Kelly: Prostitute/Police Academy recruit
Jill: Masseuse
Bosley: Manger of Paradise Massage Parlor

FACTS:
Bill Duncan, Sabrina's ex-husband is stationed in Santa Barbara, CA.
This was Jill's last "official" case with the agency.

FASHIONS:
Jill never took her clothes off but gave the best massage in Los Angeles.

STAR SIGHTING:
Joanna Kerns as Natalie.
Dirk Benedict as Barton
Michael Bell as Bill Duncan

WRITERS: Edward J. Lakso
DIRECTOR: Georg Stanford Brown
PRODUCER: Barney Rosenzweig

The Farrah Fawcett "Angels In Chains" Scrapbook

Angels it's Charlie calling... it's time to get back into those chains!!!

Here is a look back at the most loved Charlie's Angels episode.

These ULTRA RARE shots were donated by super Angel Farrah Fawcett!

Angelic Heaven

"It was the episode I remember us having the most fun." ~ Fawcett

"We got to spend more time together instead of being in the makeup chair."
~ Fawcett

"One of the easiest episodes because we did not have to worry about make-up and hair. Hair maintance was basically wetting down our hair with a spray bottle."

~ Fawcett

"Wet hair was a luxury."

~ Fawcett

"Even on break we were chained together!"
~Fawcett

Season Two

Angels:
Sabrina Duncan (Kate Jackson)
Kelly Garrett (Jaclyn Smith)
Kris Munroe (Cheryl Ladd)

Angel Airing:
ABC Wednesdays 9pm - 10pm

Angel Season Run:
September 14, 1977 - May 10, 1978

Angel Season Rating:
#4 - audience 24.4 (tied with **60 Minutes** and **All in the Family**)

Angel Episode Estimated Cost:
$390,000

Angel Opener:
Once Upon a time...there were three little girls who went to the police academy...two in Los Angeles...the other in San Francisco...and they were each assigned very hazardous duties...but I took them away from all that and now they work for me...my name is Charlie.

Angel Changes:
Jill Munroe left the agency to pursue her dream as a race car driver. The Angels are traveling with a new Angel in their midst. Her hair is not as puffy as that of Jill Munroe, but she has a striking resemblance to her. It's Jill's little sister Kris! Kris joins the team with her winning smile!

Angel Awards:
Emmy Nominated:
Kate Jackson for "Outstanding Lead Actress in a Drama Series" 1977-78

Golden Globe Awards Nominated:
Charlie's Angels for "Best TV Series - Drama" (1978)
Kate Jackson for "Best Performance by an Actress in a TV Series" (1978)

#23 - ANGELS IN PARADISE
September 14, 1977 - 2 hour episode
Kris Munroe's first case!

CASE: Kris Munroe joins the team as they fly to Hawaii to free Charlie who has been kidnapped by a woman who wants to hire the Angels to break her husband out of jail.

COVERS:
Sabrina: Herself
Kelly: Herself
Kris: Herself

FACTS:
Jill has left the Townsend Detective Agency to pursue a career in race car driving.
Mai Tais are the Angels favorite cocktail while in Hawaii.
Legendary entertainer Don Ho is a friend of Charlie's.

FASHIONS:
Kris is found on a nudist beach hiding behind a palm branch. She shines just like her older sister Jill. Welcome new Angel.

STAR SIGHTING:
Don Ho as himself
France Nuyen as Leilani Sako

TIDBIT:
Amy Carter, the daughter of the President of the United States, Jimmy Carter, stopped by to meet the Angels while on location in Hawaii.

WRITER: John D. F. Black
DIRECTOR: Charles S. Dubin
PRODUCER: Ronald Austin & James Buchanan

#24—ANGELS ON ICE
September 21, 1977 - 2 hour episode

CASE: The two lead skaters of an ice show disappear prior to the shows opening night.

COVERS:
Sabrina: Rep. Buying the skating company
Kelly: Ice Skater
Kris: Ice Skater/Clown
Bosley: Peanut Seller

FACTS:
Charlie gave the Angels ice show tickets.
Bosley loves candy apples.
Jill is the Ice skater of the family, not Kris!

FASHIONS:
Kelly looks quite fetching in her "belly-dancing" outfit!

STAR SIGHTING:
Phil Silvers as Max

WRITER: Rick Edelstein
DIRECTOR: Robert Kelljan
PRODUCER: Edward J. Lakso

#25 - PRETTY ANGELS ALL IN A ROW
(aka: Along Came a Spider)
September 28, 1977

CASE: The Miss Chrysanthemum beauty contest contestants are being mysteriously scared off and frightened.

COVERS:
Sabrina: "The Boss Lady" Reporter
Kelly: Contestant from Texas
Kris: Contestant from Georgia
Bosley: Camera Man

FACTS:
Kris is an outstanding magician seen during the "talent" competition.
Kelly dances like an Angel during her 'talent' competition
Kris and Kelly are known as "professional beauty contestants" and were not qualified to win the pageant.

FASHIONS:
Kris and Kelly are on stage in one piece swimsuits. Both Angels way-out shined the rest!

WRITER: John D.F. Black
DIRECTOR: John D.F. Black
PRODUCER: Edward J. Lakso

"ANGELS ON ICE!" SPECIAL 2-HOUR MOVIE

NEW SEASON
Someone's kidnapping ice show stars. To find out who, the Angels go underground. Kris becomes a clown skater...Kelly an exotic dancer, and with Sabrina's help, they uncover a bizarre murder plot. Starring Kate Jackson, Jaclyn Smith, Cheryl Ladd and David Doyle. Special guest star Phil Silvers as "Max."

CHARLIE'S ANGELS
abc 8:00PM ⑤ ⑦

Dancing Angels
One of the best Angel skills were their dancing feet!

- **Dancing in the Dark (#19)**
Jill plays a dance instructor
- **Angels in Paradise (#23)**
Sabrina, Kelly, Kris and Bosley find how to do the hula dance.
- **Angels on Ice (#24)**
Kelly shows it's easy to belly dance.
- **Pretty Angels All in a Row (#25)**
Kelly shows off her 'modern dance' in the beauty contest.
- **Angels in the Wings (#32)**
Kelly's dancing brings a killer out into the open as Kris dances her heart for her part in film "Sweet Misery."
- **Angels in Vegas (#47)**
Kelly makes her debut on the famous Vegas strip.
- **Disco Angels (#61)**
Kris takes after her sister Jill as an expert disco dancer.
- **Dancin' Angels - (#86)**
Bosley & Tiffany show they can dance around the ballroom very elegantly
- **Chorus Line Angels (#104)**
Kelly showcases her talent for the Broadway Stage.

#26 - ANGEL FLIGHT
October 5, 1977

CASE: Sabrina's college friend, a flight attendant, is being stalked with menacing phone calls and black roses found in obscure locations.

COVERS:
Sabrina: Old friend of Angela's
Kelly: Flight attendant trainee
Kris: Flight attendant trainee

FACTS:
Sabrina and Angela were college roommates.
Kelly can land a plane.

FASHIONS:
Kris and Kelly are found wrapped in towels. Ready to fly those friendly skies!

WRITER: Brian McKay
DIRECTOR: Dennis Donnelly
PRODUCER: Edward J. Lakso

ANGELS BECOME "STEWARDESSES" ON DEATH FLIGHT!

NEW SEASON There's a killer loose on board...no cockpit crew...and Kelly has to land the plane. Kate Jackson, Jaclyn Smith, Cheryl Ladd and David Doyle star.
CHARLIE'S ANGELS
abc 8:00PM ⑰⑲㊳

ANGELS JET INTO DANGER!

NEW SEASON The Angels pose as stewardesses to land a killer aboard a jet liner...with no pilot! Kate Jackson, Jaclyn Smith, Cheryl Ladd and David Doyle star.
CHARLIE'S ANGELS
abc 9:00PM ⑤⑧⑨⑫

Angel Fact

Kelly Garrett was the only Angel to be hit by a bullet. She had the misfortune to be shot in the head two different times.

Episodes:
To Kill an Angel (#7)
Let Our Angel Live (#109)

#27 - CIRCUS OF TERROR
October 19, 1977

CASE: The Barzak's Circus is close to bankruptcy after being plagued by numerous accidents.

COVERS:
Sabrina: A mime "in training"
Kelly: Go-Go Garrett (stunt motorcycle driver)
Kris: A showgirl

FACTS:
Sabrina falls for the Circus owner's son, David Barzak.

TIDBIT
This episode was the very first episode which Cheryl Ladd filmed after she replaced Farrah Fawcett.
Ladd also wears the "feline" costume which Fawcett wore in "Lady Killer" (#8).

WRITER: Robert Janes
DIRECTOR: Allen Baron
PRODUCER: Edward J. Lakso

#28 - ANGEL IN LOVE
October 26, 1977

CASE: The nephew of the owner of a singles resort is brutally murdered.

COVERS:
Sabrina: Writer/guest
Kelly: Ranch hand
Kris: Yoga instructor
Bosley: Guest

FACTS:
Sabrina falls in love with Doug O'Neal, one of the prime suspects.
Bosley gained 5 pounds while working on the case.
Kris showcases her lasso talent.

SIMILAR ANGEL PLOT:
#35—Angels on Horseback

FASHIONS:
Kris, Kelly and Sabrina are all found exchanging information in the hot tub. One hot case.

WRITER: Skip Webster and Jack MacKelvi
DIRECTOR: Paul Stanley
PRODUCER: Ronald Austin & James Buchanan

#29 - UNIDENTIFIED FLYING ANGELS
November 2, 1977

CASE: After a wealthy socialite disappears it blows the "spaceship" out of the air for a pair of con artist who promises "believers" contact with alien travelers.

COVERS:
Sabrina: Vice President of "United Bank"
Kelly: An alien
Kris: A kept woman
Bosley: Bank cashier/Kris' sugar daddy

FACTS:
Kelly falls for Astronaut James Britten.

FASHIONS:
Kelly is a sexy silver space alien! If aliens looked like her...outerspace would be heavenly!

STAR SIGHTING
Ross Martin as Dr. Perine
Dennis Cole as James Britten

WRITER: Ronald Austin and James Buchanan
DIRECTOR: Allen Baron
PRODUCER: Edward J. Lakso

ANGELS ON TRACK OF KILLER...FROM OUTER SPACE?
Special Tonight Only! UFO's, mysterious disappearances and the murder of a wealthy old lady put the Angels on the trail of a killer...from another world?
CHARLIE'S ANGELS
SPECIAL 8PM

International Series Titles for Charlie's Angels
As Panteras - Brazil
Droles De Dames - France
Los Angeles De Charlie - Spanish
Drei Engel Fur Charlie - German
Ba Nu Tham Tu - Vietnamese

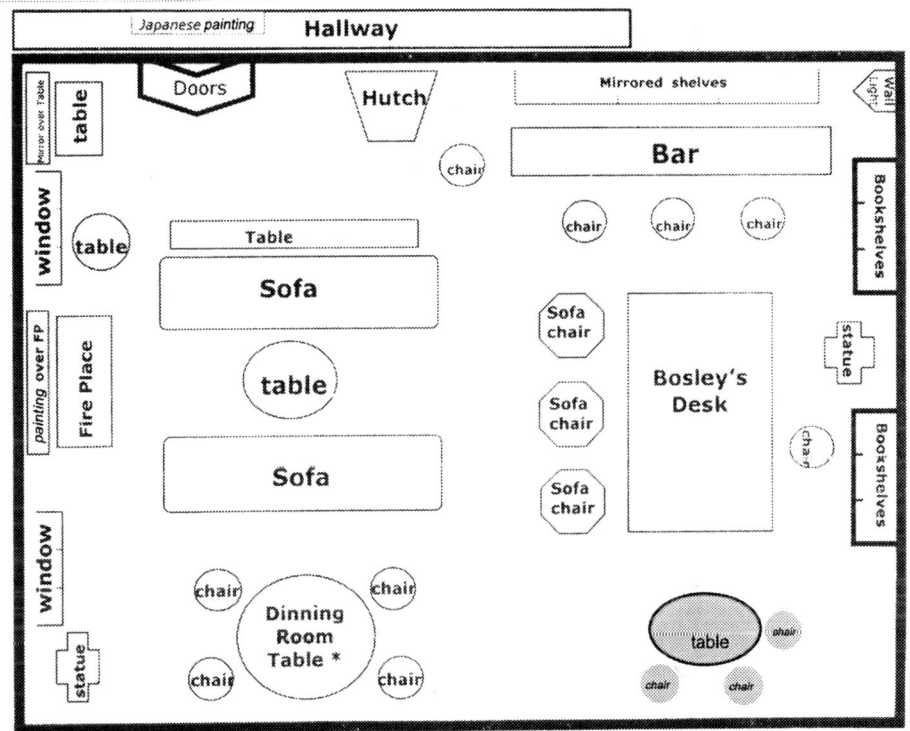

Charlie's Angels
Office Floor Plan

This is a floor plan of the Townsend Agency office. There are three areas in the office which are used the most in the series: the bar, Bosley's desk and the sofa area. Hardly used is the dining room table and chairs. This area is seen in "Circus of Terror," "Angels in the Backfield," "Angel on a Roll," and a few other episodes.

This is the floor plan which I created for the producers of the hit 2000 film **Charlie's Angels**. The set also included a kitchen and a patio area where the original dining room table was in the series.

ANGELS TAKE TO AIRWAVES TO TRACK DOWN KILLER!

The Angels join a station's news staff to head off the murder of a beautiful reporter. Starring Kate Jackson, Jaclyn Smith, Cheryl Ladd.

CHARLIE'S ANGELS 9:00 PM

#30 - ANGELS ON THE AIR
November 9, 1977

CASE: A female radio investigator reporter is the target for murder.

COVERS:
Sabrina: "Skylark" reporter/student
Kelly: Joy Vance
Kris: Girl biker
Bosley: News assignment editor

FACTS:
Kris can ride a Harley.

FASHIONS:
Kris looking good in her biker attire.

WRITER: William Frong
DIRECTOR: George Brooks
PRODUCER: Ronald Austin & James Buchanan

#31- ANGEL BABY
November 16, 1977

CASE: A friend of Kelly's goes AWOL in order to find his girlfriend who has disappeared.

COVERS:
Sabrina: Mrs Bosley/Buyer of Kelly's child
Kelly: Pregnant woman from Beaumont, Texas
Kris: Prostitute
Bosley: A millionaire

FACTS:
This episode holds the emotional scene in which Kris shoots a person for the very first time.

TIDBITS:
In this episode Sabrina and Bosley play husband and wife. Interesting to note that Sabrina is smoking in this episode since she is deathly against smoking in "Magic Fire" (#33).

WRITER: George R. Hodges and John D.F. Black
STORY BY: George R. Hodges
DIRECTOR: Paul Stanley
PRODUCER: Ronald Austin & James Buchanan

KELLY POSES AS UNWED MOTHER!

The Angels investigate a murder and discover a shocking traffic in black market babies.

CHARLIE'S ANGELS 9:00 PM

Employee Angel Card: **Sabrina Duncan**

Born: Philadelphia, Pennsylvania

Family: Father, a General in the Army

Schooling: 1975 -graduated from the Los Angeles Police Academy.

Address: Apartment in Los Angeles, CA

Employment: Townsend Detective Agency, Los Angeles 1976-1979

Current: Housewife 1979-present

Nickname: Brie

Pets: none

Boyfriends: Jim Taylor (#2), Tony Mann (#8), Peter Wychinski (#15), David Barzak (#27), Doug O'Neal (#28), Frank Howell (#47)

Marriage: Divorced in 1975 from — Bill Duncan; Married second time — 1979 with a child

Best Friends: Kelly Garrett, Jill Munroe, Kris Munroe, John Bosley —associates at the Townsend Agency, Angela (#26) - old college friend.

Car: Ford Pinto — Orange/red color -company car

Interests: Race car driving, football, bilingual, horse back riding, skiing

Best Detective Skills: A master of characters and being "The Smart One"

Angelic Heaven

#32—ANGELS IN THE WINGS
November 23, 1977

CASE: A movie set haults production of "Sweet Misery," after a series of mishaps threaten the lives of the cast and crew.

COVERS:
Sabrina: Herself
Kelly: Actor/dancer
Kris: Actress in musical

FACTS:
Kris got received reviews in Summer Stock Theatre

TIDBITS:
This episode used Sound Stage #8 as backdrop where the musical "Sweet Misery" was being filmed. In reality Sound Stage #8 located on the 20th Century lot was the real sound stage where **Charlie's Angels** was filmed every week!
This was the first time Kris sings & dances on a case. The song she sings is called, "IF ONLY WE'D BEEN TOGETHER THEN" with guest star Gene Barry. All the music show stoppers were written by Angel producer/writer veteran, Edward J. Lakso. Lakso also was the writer and producer of this Angel musical.

FASHIONS:
Angels seem to keep their clothes on but Kris can really belt out a tune while dancing her Angelic heart out!

STAR SIGHTINGS:
Shani Wallis as Ellen Jason
Gene Barry as Frank Jason

SIMILAR EPISODE:
#105 - Stuntwomen Angels

WRITER: Edward J. Lakso
DIRECTOR: Dennis Donnelly
PRODUCER: Edward J. Lakso

#33 - MAGIC FIRE
November 30, 1977

CASE: A string of arsons are taking place and believed to be the work of a professional magician known as the "Magic Man."

COVERS:
Sabrina: Maxine Myntie, a Paris Designer
Kelly: Elizabeth Hart, daughter of a magician
Kris: Zolton's Assistant
Bosley: The Great Zolton

FACTS:
Jaclyn's dog, Albert makes another "Angel" appearance.

FASHIONS:
Kris narrowly escapes stepping into a really hot shower full of shooting flames.

TIDBITS
While the Angels were filming this episode they had a visitor on the set, the charming and very single (at the time) Prince Charles.
Parts of the episode were filmed at the Magic Castle in Los Angeles, CA.
As Kelly's car leaves the Magic Castle, look closely at the driver and the passengers. It's three male stand-ins posing as the Angels.

WRITER: Lee Sheldon
DIRECTOR: Leon Carrere
PRODUCER: Ronald Austin & James Buchanan

ANGELS SCREEN CLUES IN HOLLYWOOD MURDERS!
Kris takes a role in a movie musical as the Angels investigate a series of deadly accidents on a Hollywood sound stage.
CHARLIE'S ANGELS
abc 9:00PM 7 8

#34 - SAMMY DAVIS JR. KIDNAP CAPER
December 7, 1977

CASE: The Angels are hired after several attempts are made to kidnap Sammy Davis Jr.

COVERS:
Sabrina: Chairperson on the committee for giving
Kelly: Model
Kris: Reporter for "On the Spot News"
Bosley: Camera man/chauffeur

STAR SIGHTING
Sammy Davis Jr. as himself & look-alike Herbert Brubaker III
Norman Alden as Louis Fluellen
Altovise Davis as herself
Robert Pine as Andy Price
Martin Kove as Georgie

TIDBIT:
The gold dress Jaclyn wears at the end of the episode is the dress Jaclyn wears on her apperance on **The Love Boat** and on **ABC's Silver Anniversary Special.**

WRITER: Ron Friedman
DIRECTOR: Ronald Austin
PRODUCER: Ronald Austin & James Buchanan

77

Angelic Heaven

Angel Fact:
Cheryl Ladd was the only Angel to actually sing on the series! In episodes **Angels in the Wings** (#32) & **Angels in Vegas** (#47)!

#35 - ANGELS ON HORSEBACK
December 21, 1977

CASE: While aboard a bus en route to a dude ranch, a man is mysteriously killed.

COVERS:
Sabrina: Guest From Beaut Montana
Kelly: Guest, from Philadelphia/Divorce
Kris: Guest from Demoines, Iowa
Bosley: Guest from Chicago/Pharmaceutics Rep.

FACTS:
After riding old saw tooth Bosely had to be raulfed (deep tissue massage).

TIDBITS:
Felise's boutique is also used in "Angel Baby" (#31).
The Dude Ranch was a set also used on "Fantasy Island."

SIMILAR EPISODES:
#28 - Angel In Love

FASHIONS:
Kris and Kelly are trying on their sexy new bathing suits in the boutique.

Writer: Edward J. Lakso
Director: George W. Brooks
Producer: Edward J. Lakso

Broadway Garrett!
In several episodes, Jaclyn Smith uses her background in dancing.

The Vegas Connection (#17)
Pretty Angels In A Row (#25)
Angels In The Wings (#32)
Angels In Vegas (#47)
Chorus Line Angels (#104)

Prostitute Angels

Consenting Adults - (#10)
Jill, a high-paid call girl finds her first client to be good-old Bosley!

The Blue Angels - (#22)
Jill & Sabrina find themselves working in the massage parlors in Venice, CA is a deadly way to go.

The Vegas Connection - (#17)
Kelly, a Vegas dancer needing extra cash, might not be a pro; however she is a gifted amateur!

Little Angels of the Night - (#43)
Sabrina, Kelly & Kris go undercover as "working girls" in an apartment building, they never seem to work!

Angels on the Street - (#75)
Tiffany & Kelly work the street of Los Angeles as a "Team." The cost? $1,000 each!

Employee Angel Card: **Kris Munroe**

Born: Los Angeles, CA

Family: Sister — Jill Munroe; Aunt & Uncle (#59), an alcoholic father (#87)

Schooling: 1977 - Graduated from the San Francisco Police Academy

Address: Malibu Beach, CA

Employment: Townsend Detective Agency, Los Angeles 1977-present

Nickname: None

Pets: None

Boyfriends: Ted Markham (#38), Dave Christopher (#40), Paul Halister (#69), Bill Cord (#92-93)

Marriage: Single

Best Friends: Kelly Garrett, Sabrina Duncan, Tiffany Welles, Julie Rogers, John Bosely Linda Frye (#51) - old school friend

Car: Los Angeles - Ford Cobra - white w/Blue Strip — company car;
Hawaii: Chevrolet Z28 Covert -Brown car - company car

Interests: Hang gliding, singing, magic, rollerskating, disco dancing, yoga, tennis

Best Detective Skills: A rookie way of thinking.

#36—GAME, SET, DEATH
January 4, 1978

CASE: A tennis racket promoter tries to make his fleeting tennis star a winner again by killing off the competition.

COVERS:
Sabrina: Clothing Designer
Kelly: Model
Kris: Tennis Pro
Bosley: Cushion Boy

FACTS:
Kris played Tennis in College.
Bosley has a heavy date with Ms. Halley

TIDBITS:
Kris mentions that she played tennis in college; however, Kris never went to college. She went to the Police Academy. Look for the reverse image of the Angels during the slide show presentation.

FASHIONS:
After Kris's match, she is found strutting in an orange terry cloth towel.

Writer: Worley Thorne
Director: George Stanford Brown
Producer: Edward J. Lakso

#37—HOURS OF DESPERATION
January 11, 1978

CASE: Two crooks are double crossed by their partner after a diamond heist. The crooks take Sabrina & Bosley hostage and place an explosive belt around Sabrina's waist forcing Kelly & Kris to find their missing diamonds.

COVERS:
Sabrina: Herself
Kelly: Herself
Kris: "Cindy Bundette" a singer

FACTS:
Kelly once again showcases her expertise in picking locks.

FASHIONS:
Kelly is steaming it up in a towel and in a steam box.

TIDBITS:
Watch in the background for the hutch doors in the office to open and close by themselves throughout the episode.

Writer: Ray Brenner
Director: Cliff Bole
Producer: Edward J. Lakso

Sabrina's Best Characters

Angels on a String (#15)
Plays a clumsy waitress
Dancing in the Dark (#19)
Plays an heiress
Counterfeit Angels (#60)
Doing a continuing impression of herself
Magic Fire (#33)
Plays Maxine Myntie
The Sandcastle Murders (#40)
Plays a bum

#38—DIAMOND IN THE ROUGH
January 18, 1978

CASE: A renowned cat burglar enlist the Angels help to find the diamond he's accused of stealing.

COVERS:
Sabrina: Lady Brander
Kelly: Secretary
Kris: Masseuse
Bosley: Butler

FACTS:
Charlie sent "Freddy the Fox" a well known diamond thief to jail

FASHIONS:
Kris is showing off her personal jewels in a one piece brown bathing suit at the Tycoons' Birthday party.

Writer: Brian MacKay, Ronald Austin, James Buchanan
Story by: Brian McKay
Director: Ronald Austin
Producer: Ronald Austin & James Buchanan

#39 - ANGELS IN THE BACKFIELD
January 25, 1978

CASE: An all womans football team is receiving threatening phone calls and are terrorized by a band of motorcyclists.

COVERS:
Sabrina: Football player #1
Kelly: Football player #33
Kris: Football player #88

FACTS:
During their Police Academy years, Sabrina played Quarterback & Kelly played running back on the Academy's football team.

STAR SIGHTING
L.Q. Jones as Dan Jarvis
Nancy Fox as Amy Jarvis

FASHIONS:
These team players looking heavenly in towels during the all woman shower scene.

Writer: Edward J. Lakso
Director: Ronald Austin
Producer: Edward J. Lakso

MEET THE NEW FOOTBALL STARS ...THE FIGHTING ANGELS!

The Angels tackle a bunch of crooks who are trying to knock a women's football team out of the game! Starring Kate Jackson, Jaclyn Smith, Cheryl Ladd, David Doyle.
CHARLIE'S ANGELS
9:00 PM

#40 - THE SANDCASTLE MURDERS
(aka: Sandcastles)
February 1, 1978

CASE: A killer covers his victims bodies with sandcastles in a rash of murders.

COVERS:
Sabrina: Bag Lady
Kelly: Herself
Kris: Herself
Bosley: Cook

FACTS:
The Angels have planned a party and some of the players from the RAMS are expected to attend.

FASHION:
Kris is home alone reading a book in a sexy blue bath robe.

STAR SIGHTING:
Melody Thomas Scott as Besty

Writer: Wkip Webster, Jack MacKelvie, Robert Dennis, Ronald Autin and James Buchanan
Director: George McCowan
Producers: Ronald Austin & James Buchanan

RICH BEAUTY MURDERED! ANGELS SET TRAP FOR KILLER!

A beautiful millionairess plays with fire when she plays with a young playboy. And now the Angels have to smoke out a killer! Kate Jackson, Jaclyn Smith, Cheryl Ladd, David Doyle star.
CHARLIE'S ANGELS
8 PM

ANGELS MAKE THE COUNTRY MUSIC SCENE... TO FIND A KILLER!

The Angels investigate the mysterious death of a country-western star...and uncover a shocking secret about her life! Starring Kate Jackson, Jaclyn Smith, Cheryl Ladd, David Doyle.
CHARLIE'S ANGELS
ABC 8:00PM 9 11 12

#41 - ANGEL BLUES
(aka: Angel in the Night)
February 8, 1978

CASE: A country singer and ex-drug addict mysteriously overdoses on heroine.

COVERS:
Sabrina: Herself
Kelly: Herself
Kris: Reporter for "Country Music Quarterly"
Bosley: Editor

FACTS:
Sabrina's license plate number is CA 846RUZ. Singer Amy Waters is one of Charlie's favorites singers.

TIDBIT:
The song used in this episode was titled "Trippin' to the Mornin" sung by Lynn Marta and was written by Edward J. Lakso.

Writer: Edward J. Lakso
Director: George Stanford Brown
Producer: Edward J. Lakso

Lovestories
Season Two

Circus of Terror
(episode #27)
Sabrina falls in love with the Angels client, David Barzak. Sabrina finds herself in many lip locks and love in her eyes! After the clown paint was gone so was Barzak.

Circus of Terror
(episode #27)
Bosley tries to run away from the affections of Tinkerbell. Tinkerbell finds "Bosley, John Bosley" her true Angel. Size does matter!

Unidentified Flying Angels
(episode #29)
Kelly, the Alien Angel, falls for Astronaut, James Britten (Dennis Cole). After Britten tries to kill Kelly there are no more dates for him again!

Diamond in the Rough
(episode #38)
Kris Munroe begins to show affections for the son of the man who stole a priceless diamond. Love shines after all when he lets Kris and the Angels getaway with the diamond.

The Jade Trap
(episode #44)
Kelly is purring as she falls for Ted Machlin, the cat burglar. After the cat is out of the bag, Kelly can't help but wonder if she will ever find the right guy.

Antique Angels
(episode #46)
The Angels search for a "space age fuel" at an Antique Car Show. Bosley's roaming eyes glaze upon a beautiful woman. He finds he has more Angelic values than becoming her "kept man"!

#42—MOTHER GOOSE IS RUNNING FOR HIS LIFE
February 15, 1978

CASE: After the owner of a toy company is unwilling to sell his company, many unexplained accidents began to occur.

COVERS:
Sabrina: Jennifer Collins from Hong Kong
Kelly: Professional wiretapper
Kris: Model/large rag doll
Bosley: Attorney

FACT:
Kelly asks to get a set of dolls for her niece, however she's an orphan!
Kris still owns a stuffed Kola bear.

TIDBITS:
Angels are presented with their real "Charlie's Angels" dolls at the end of this episode!
This is the episode where Kris is dressed up as a large "raggedy" doll!

FASHIONS:
Kris looks great modeling a hang glider in a very small tank top! Happy Flying!

Writer: Del Reisman, Ronald Austin, James Buchanan
Director: George McCowan
Producer: Ronald Austin & James Buchanan

ANGELS IN TOYLAND PLAY A DEADLY GAME!

The Angels investigate a strange murder at the "Mother Goose Toy Company"...and almost get theirs cooked! Kate Jackson, Jaclyn Smith, Cheryl Ladd, David Doyle star.
CHARLIE'S ANGELS
②⑨:00PM ⑦⑧

TOP 10 KIDNAPPING:

10. Avenging Angel (#71):
While drugged up on heroine, Kelly is kidnapped and held hostage in a warehouse.

9. Bullseye (#9):
Tied-up & AWOL! Jill's Army career was shortened as she's kidnapped and held in a hanger.

8. Angels on the Air (#30):
Bound & truth needles! Sabrina's a guinea pig as a student researcher who is bound & gagged.

7 Angels on Campus (#78):
Mail Order Bride! Tiffany revisits her college years to become the next victim to be sold into slavery.

6. Hula Angels (#99):
Dancing Cage! Julie's dancing gets her kidnapped and held in a cage in a warehouse.

5. An Angel's Trail (#88):
Of Mice and Men! Jill's kidnapping is like the cliffnotes of the Steinbeck novel retold in this modern day, Angelic retelling "Of Mice and Men".

4. Angel in a Box (#63):
Decoy Angel! Kris is kidnapped and Jill is forced to find out what it's like to lose someone you love.

3. Pom Pom Angels (#53):
Printing Ink and Pom Poms! Kris is kidnapped by a religious freak and taken a print mill to be inducted into "The Good One's" harem or better known as "I hate long hair" kidnapping club.

2. Toni Boy's (#91):
Boy Angels! The male version of the Angels! Kelly, Kris and Tiffany are kidnapped in a bad reenactment of Edgar Allan Poe's "The Cask of Amontillado", as the Angels are being sealed (via brick) in a wine cellar.

1. Angels in Paradise (#23):
Flip-Flop Kidnapping! In beautiful Hawaii Charlie is kidnapped twice while in the lap of luxury, forcing the Angels to fly to paradise to find him.

Angelic Heaven

ANGELS BECOME SHADY LADIES TO LURE KILLER!

The Angels go undercover in the twilight world of vice to discover why three beautiful call girls have been murdered. Kate Jackson, Jaclyn Smith, Cheryl Ladd, David Doyle star.

CHARLIE'S ANGELS
abc 9:00 PM ④

KRIS ACTS AS BAIT TO HOOK KILLER!

Unless the Angels stop a strangler obsessed with blonde, blue-eyed women...Kris will be his next victim.

CHARLIE'S ANGELS
abc 9:00 PM ⑤

#43—LITTLE ANGELS OF THE NIGHT
(aka: The Play for Pay Girls)
February 22, 1978

CASE: "Working Girls" are targets for murder at an apartment building for call girls.

COVERS:
Sabrina: Prostitute from Chicago
Kelly: Prostitute from Chicago
Kris: Prostitute from Chicago
Bosley: Janitor

FACTS:
Charlie and Dolly Smith's "relationship" goes back for a very long time. Dolly Smith owns the apartment building in which the working girls live.

FASHIONS:
Angels are bathing beauties in their bathing suits by the pool.

SIMILAR EPISODE:
#61 Disco Angels

TIDBIT:
This is the episode that holds a high speed chase on bikes!

Writer: Mickey Rose
Director: George Stanford Brown
Producer: Edward J. Lakso

Season Two Opening Sequence (1977-1978)

1. Police Academy Shot
2. Sabrina at police firing range
3. Kelly in police defense class
4. Kris S.F.P.D. driver training
5. Sabrina a police parking attendant
6. Kelly a police crosswalk guard
7. Kris on the police phone switch board
8. Sabrina & Kelly walking out of Police Department and Kris joins them
9. Silhouette Angel with Walkie-Talkie and lettering "Kate Jackson"
10. Race Car Driving - Episode "Hellride"
11. Sabrina at the office bar - Episode "Angels in Paradise"
12. Sabrina Running - Episode "Pilot Film"
13. Sabrina squatting - Episode "Pilot Film"
14. Sabrina clapping her hands - Episode "Angels in Paradise"
15. Silhouette Angel Karate Chopping and lettering "Jaclyn Smith"
16. Kelly running from her car - Episode "Angels on Wheels"
17. Kelly on motor cycle - Episode "Pilot Film"
18. Kelly taking a photo with camera - Episode "The Killing Kind"
19. Kelly doing a turn and putting on a hat - Episode "Night of the Strangler"
20. Kelly with head over shoulder - Episode "The Killing Kind"
21. Silhouette Angel with Gun and lettering "Cheryl Ladd"
22. Kris is running in blue jump suit - (unkownn episode)
23. Kris in a magic show - Episode "Pretty Angels All in a Row"
24. Kris on boat in bathing suit - Episode "Angels in Paradise"
25. Kris having knives thrown at her - Episode "Circus of Terror"
26. Kris in a hot tub - Episode "Angel in Love"
27. Silhouette of Bosley and lettering "David Doyle"
28. Bosley hugging Sabrina - Episode "Hellrider"
29. Bosley handing a gift - Episode "Hellrider"
30. Charlie's Angles Logo and Exploding

Angel Fact:
Two of today's mega super-stars were up for leading roles on **Charlie's Angels**! Kim Basinger was up to replace Farrah Fawcett and Michelle Pfeiffer was almost the replacement for Kate Jackson!

#44— THE JADE TRAP
(aka: Diamonds are an Angels Best Friend)
March 1, 1978

CASE: A wealthy woman is murdered during a series of jewel robberies at a residential hotel.

COVERS:
Sabrina: Herself
Kelly: Kelly Devero from New Orleans/Kelly King
Kris: Onaka Bjornbar from Switzerland
Bosley: Auctioneer

FACTS:
Charlie owns the expensive Jade collection which is used as a trap to capture the jewel thief; but during an auction, Bosley sells the Jade off to a real buyer! Kelly falls in love with the jewel thief, Ted Machlin.

FASHIONS:
Kris is almost caught snooping around the murderer's boat in very tight shorts. She sure can sail!

STAR SIGHTING:
Barry Bostwick as Ted Machlin
Dirk Benedict as Denny Railsback

Written: Lee Sheldon
Director: George McCown
Producer: Ronald Austin & James Buchanan

#45 - ANGELS ON THE RUN
March 5, 1978

CASE: A dump truck driver ends up missing after stolen diamonds are thrown into the back of his truck.

COVERS:
Sabrina: Hick neighbor
Kelly: Sue Cantrell
Kris: Hick neighbor
Bosley: Hick neighbor

STAR SIGHTING:
Judy Landers as Mrs. Chicken
Craig T. Nelson as Stone

TIDBITS:
This episode holds the famous scene of John Bosley trying to buy his "chicken breasts" from Mrs. Chicken played by actress Judy Landers. This was the first time Judy Landers played the comic slapstick with David Doyle. Later she will be seen again as the "Linen Lady" in the episode "Love Boat Angels" (#69).

Written: Edward J. Lakso
Director: Robert Kelljan
Producer: Ronald Austin & James Buchanan

#46—ANTIQUE ANGELS
Last episode of 2nd season
March 10, 1978

CASE: Stolen space age fuel leads the Angels to an antique car show and a cast of on-edge suspects.

COVERS:
Sabrina: American Antique Car Magazine Reporter
Kelly: American Antique Car Magazine Reporter
Kris: American Antique Car Magazine Reporter
Bosley: American Antique Car Magazine Reporter

FACTS:
Bosley had a date
Kris's hat does not fit

FASHIONS:
Angels are very fashionable in the period costumes as "Key Stone Cops."

TIDBIT:
Kris's "Key-Stone Cop" hat is too big for her head!

Writer: Lea Travis & Edward J. Lakso
Director: Leon Carrere
Producer: Edward J. Lakso

RICH BEAUTY MURDERED! ANGELS SET TRAP FOR KILLER!

A beautiful millionairess plays with fire when she plays with a young playboy. And now the Angels have to smoke out a killer! Kate Jackson, Jaclyn Smith, Cheryl Ladd, David Doyle star.
CHARLIE'S ANGELS
ABC 8PM

Angels in Paradise Scrapbook

*Photos courtesy
of
Cynthia A. Lai*

Angelic Heaven

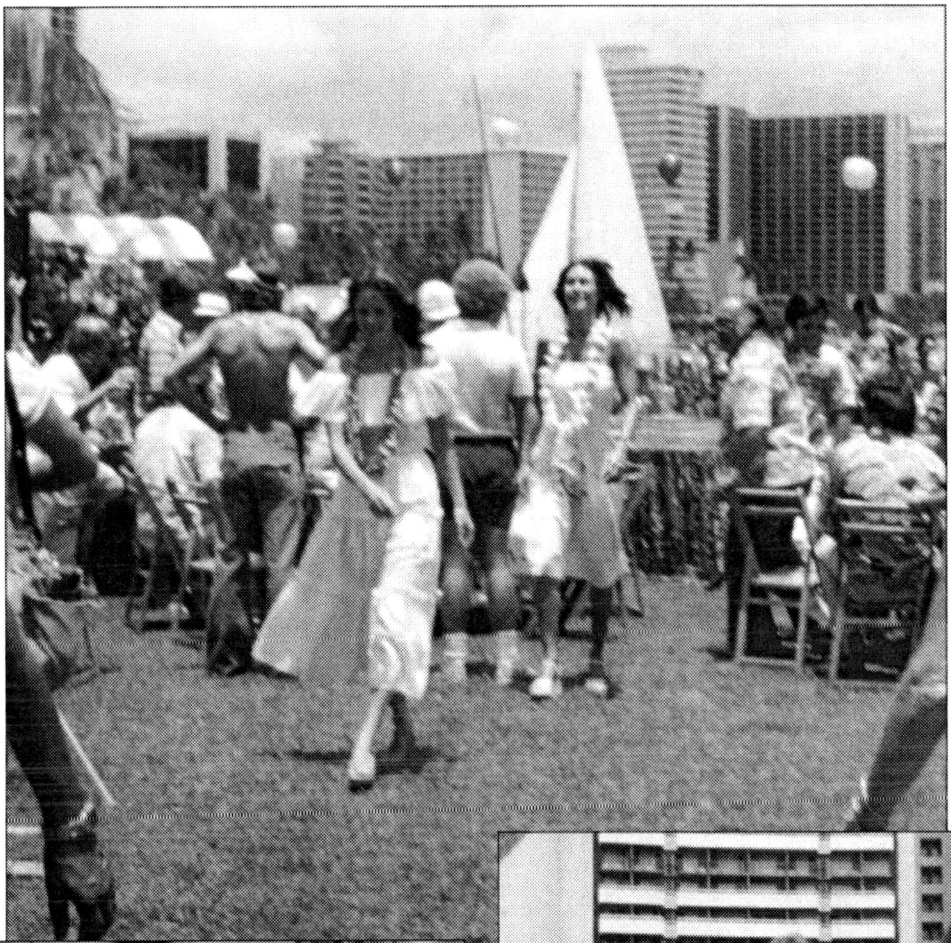

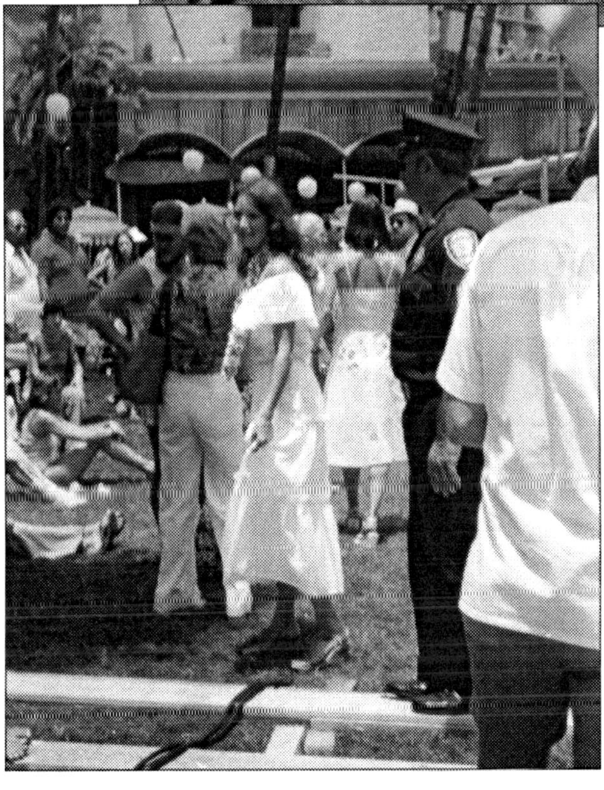

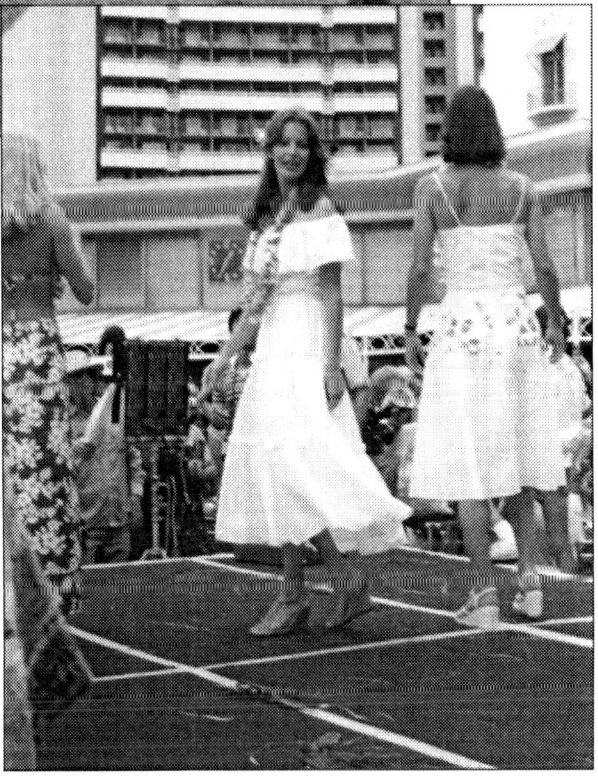

Angelic Heaven

91

Season Three

Angels:
Sabrina Duncan (Kate Jackson)
Kelly Garrett (Jaclyn Smith)
Kris Munroe (Cheryl Ladd)
Jill Munroe (Farrah Fawcett)

Angel Airing:
ABC Wednesdays
9pm - 10pm

Angel Season Run:
September 13, 1978 -
May 16, 1979

Angel Season Rating:
#12 - audience 24.4

Angel Episode Estimated Cost:
$440,000

Angel Opener:
Once upon a time...there were three little girls who went to the police academy...two in Los Angeles...the other in San Francisco...and they each assigned very hazardous duties...but I took them away from all that and now they work for me...my name is Charlie.

Angel Found:
Jill Munroe returns to the office for three more cases.

Angel Changes:
This is the only season that the office staff stayed the same!

Angel Awards:
Golden Globe Awards Nominated:
Kate Jackson for "Best Performance by an Actress in a TV Series" (1979)

Angel Overview:
Kris, Kelly and Sabrina are very happy for a second year solving crime together. Sabrina gets a new hairdo and the office gets a new paint job and a new rug! In the wings, Jill Munroe is waiting to help the Angels with three new cases.

#47—ANGELS IN VEGAS
3rd season 2hr opener
September 13, 1978

CASE: A club singer has resentful feelings toward a casino owner who he blames for the death of his beloved wife.

COVERS:
Sabrina: Franks personal consultant
Kelly: Dancer from Dallas
Kris: Night club singer
Bosley: Valet

FACTS:
Sabrina gets a new hairstyle.
Sabrina falls in love with Frank Howell.
Kris can drive a high speed boat.

STAR SIGHTING
Dean Martin as Frank Howell
Dick Sargent as Marty Cole
Robert Urich as Dan Tanna
Lee Travis as Joan Wells
Scatman Crothers as Gyb Baker

TIDBITS:
This episode introduces Angel fans to Spelling-Goldberg's newest series "Vegas" and the sexy actor, Robert Urich.

Writer: Edward J. Lakso
Director: Robert Kelljan
Producer: Edward J. Lakso

#48—ANGEL COME HOME
(aka: Angels on Fire)
Jill' first return episode
September 20, 1978

CASE: Jill returns home after receiving an urgent cablegram believed to be from her sister Kris.

COVERS:
Sabrina: Photographer
Jill: Herself
Kelly: Reporter for "Insider Magazine."
Kris: Herself

FACTS
Bosley keeps a scrap book on Jill.
Jill is engaged to Steve Carmody.
Steve Carmody is killed in an exploding car meant for Jill.
Kelly & Sabrina play a mean backgammon game.
Bosley closes the office to cheer Jill up -- A First!

FASHIONS:
Kris is in a one piece bathing suit standing next to her sexy sister Jill. Great genes.

STAR SIGHTING:
Farrah Fawcett as Jill Munroe
Stephen Collins as Steve Carmody

Written: Stephen Kandel
Director: Paul Stanley
Producer: Ronald Austin & James Buchanan

Angel Fact:
Farrah Fawcett and Cheryl Ladd played the "Munroe" sisters in the series.

#49—ANGELS ON HIGH
September 27, 1978

CASE: A dying tycoon wants to find out if he has a son.

COVERS:
Angels: Themselves

FACTS:
Kelly falls in love with Bill Freedman.
Kelly flies an airplane.

FASHIONS:
Kris finds herself having lunch in a bikini with the bad guys! I hope they paid for lunch.

TIDBIT:
Notice the tight close-ups of Cheryl in her bikini. The swimsuit was so small, they had to zoom in on Cheryl's face in order to not show "all of her." That Little Rebel. This was in response to Aaron Spelling's request that Cheryl wear more bikinis.

Writer: Edward J. Lakso
Director: Larry Doheny
Producer: Edward J. Lakso

#50—ANGELS IN SPRINGTIME
October 10, 1978

CASE: A Broadway star is murdered at the Springtime Spa by her best friend over a book of memoires which was partly based on their lifetime of feuding friendship.

COVERS:
Sabrina: Dietitian
Kelly: Wealthy guest
Kris: Exercise instructor
Bosley: Electrician

FACTS:
Charlie acted with Eve Le Deux in "A Midsummer Night Dream"

FASHIONS:
The Angels in the steam room discussing the case and they make the steam rise! Wow it's getting hot!

TIDBITS:
Kelly mentions she can not be hypnotized due to previous experience. Referring back to the episode "The Seance" (#11) when she was hypnotized and almost kills Jill and herself.

STAR SIGHTING
Amy Stryker as Eve Perkins
Marie Windsor as Eve Le Deux
Nancy Parson as Zora

Writer: William Froug
Director: Larry Stewart
Producer: Ronald Austin & James Buchanan

Death a Knocking!
Throughout the years the Angels had to fake their own deaths to get out of some deadly cases:

Target: Angels (#5)
Sabrina throws her own funeral after she is supposedly dead after an exploding water jug accident.

The Big Tap Out (#14)
Jill gets hit by a speeding car.

Angel Hunt (#79)
Tiffany is knocked unconscience and left to drown.

heavenly memory
Cheryl Ladd on wresting an "alligator" in episode "Winning Is For Losers"

"I vaguely remember filming that scene. I think the alligator was rubber, my stunt double shot most of that scene. I was probably in my trailer doing my nails!" (laughs) ~ Cheryl Ladd

#51—WINNING IS FOR LOSERS
October 18, 1978

CASE: Kris best friend Linda has had her life threatened making her drop out of a golf tournament.

COVERS:
ANGELS: bodyguards/guests

FACTS:
Linda and Kris are best friends.
Linda & Kris took an Acapulco vacation together in 1974.
Linda & Kris exchange Christmas cards every year.
KBEX jacket is also used in episode #30.
Kelly plays golf.

STAR SIGHTING:
Jamie Lee Curtis plays Linda Frye
Casey Kasem as Tom Rogers

TIDBITS:
This is one of the more well known episodes in which Kris wrestles with a live alligator.
Sabrina runs out of the hotel room without a gun to find the person who threw a rock in the window. When she arrives outside the hotel, she is holding her gun. After she can't find anyone outside, Sabrina walks back in the room without her gun in hand. Now you see it, now you don't.
Sharp shooter, Kelly doesn't know what a gun patch is - so Sabrina has to explain it to her.

Writer: Ray Brenner
Director: Cliff Bole
Producer: Edward J. Lakso

Death stalks the Angels in a haunted mansion!
CHARLIE'S ANGELS
9:00 PM

#52—HAUNTED ANGELS
October 25, 1978

CASE: Bosley's good friend is being swindled out of her money from a psychic research institute.

COVERS:
Sabrina: Subject with psychic powers
Kelly: Detective
Kris: Research grad student

FACTS:
Bosley and his friend Claire have been bridge partners for three years.

Writer: Lee Sheldon
Director: Ronald Austin
Producer: Ronald Austin & James Buchanan

#53—POM POM ANGELS
November 1, 1978

CASE: Cheerleaders disappear after the team starts receiving threatening letters. "The Good One," a religious kook, wants to lead these cheerleaders from their evil ways.

COVERS:
Sabrina: Cheerleader coach
Kelly: Cheerleader
Kris: Cheerleader
Bosley: Larry, electronic/talent agent

FACTS:
Sabrina was a cheerleader in college.
Charlie gives the Angels a vacation on a cruise as a bonus for a case well done.

FASHIONS:
Kris and Kelly looking too good with their pom poms.

Writer: Richard Carr
Director: Cliff Bole
Producer: Edward J. Lakso

#54—Angels Ahoy
November 8, 1978

CASE: A passenger was killed on a cruise ship which is being used to smuggle criminals out of the country by the cruise ship staff.

COVERS:
Sabrina: Sabrina Lampone, criminal
Kelly: Activity director
Kris: Wealthy passenger
Bosley: Passenger

FACTS:
Bosley is known as "saltan of slam" of ping pong.
Bosley says he was never been married but in The Killing Kind (#6) he refers to his wife.

FASHIONS:
Kris dressed up as Little Bo Peep! Who would not want to be in her flock?

Writer: Lee Sheldon
Director: Allen Baron
Producer: Ronald Austin & James Buchanan

HIGH SEAS ADVENTURE! A mysterious disappearance leads the Angels into a storm of intrigue!
CHARLIE'S ANGELS
7PM
8PM

Employee Angel Card: John Bosley

Born: Los Angeles, CA
Address: Los Angeles Home
Employment: Townsend Detective Agency, Los Angeles 1976-present
Nickname: Boz
Pets: Cocker Spaniel
Marital Status: Yes
Best Friends: Charles, Jill, Kelly, Sabrina, Kris, Tiffany, Julie, Claire (#52)
Car: Los Angeles: Black station wagon & Green Ford-Lincoln
Interests: Food, paperwork, dollars and cents
Best Detective Skills: Just being Bosley

Employee Angel Card: Charles Townsend*

Born: Los Angeles, CA
Address: 674 Vinewood Lane
Business:
 Townsend Detective Agency,
 --Los Angeles 1976-present
 Venus Trucking (#70) 1979-present
Nickname: Charlie
Pets: none
Marriage: Divorced. Name Unknown
Best Friends: John Bosley, The Angels, Gloria Gibson (#20), Dolly Smith (#43), Chadway (#62), and Tiffany's Father (#69)
Interests: Women
Best Detective Skills: Having Angels work for him and having friends in all the right places.

```
      *no photo available at this time,
              Sorry Angels.
```

Townsend Detective Agency Office Information

Los Angeles Address:
193 Robertson, Los Angeles, CA
Phone Number: 213.555.0267
Private Line: 213.555.9626
Company Cars: Green Ford-Lincoln
                  Black Station Wagon
Hawaii: Address:
4376 Kahaii Ave Honolulu, Hawaii

#55—MOTHER ANGEL
Jill's second return
November 15, 1978

CASE: An imaginative little girl witnesses a murder in the apartment next door with no one believing her. She calls on Jill for help.

COVERS:
Sabrina: Maid "Katie McGuire"
Jill: Herself
Kelly: "Kelly O'Tulip" Flower Association
Kris: Herself

FACTS:
Jill came in third at Lamanz.
Charlie has had relations with the girl's Aunt Charlotte.
Jill is a friend of the girls Aunt Charlotte.
Bosley has a cocker spaniel.

FASHIONS:
Jill wears a dark blue terry cloth towel while she baby-sits. Jill wants to be your baby-sitter!

STAR SIGHTING:
Gary Collins as Victor Buckley
Olivia Barash as Sam Antha

TIDBIT:
Watch for Farrah's hair swinging backwards as she notices someone looking at her through the window.

Writer: Rift Fournier
Director: Don Chaffey
Producer: Ronald Austin & James Buchanan

#56—ANGEL ON MY MIND
November 22, 1978

CASE: Kris stumbles onto a murder. The killer hits Kris with his car and she ends up with amnesia.

COVERS:
Themselves

FACTS:
Bosley picks up the restaurant check.
Kris got a new jacket, purse and scarf.
Kris has an appointment with her hair dresser.

FASHIONS:
Not too many fashion changes, but Kris did lose her memory!!

STAR SIGHTING:
Jonathan Frakes as Brad

TIDBIT:
Cheryl Ladd's real life daughter, Jordan Ladd plays Kris Munroe as a child in a flashback.

Writer: Edward J. Lakso
Director: Curtis Harrington
Producer: Edward J. Lakso

#57—ANGELS BELONG IN HEAVEN
December 6, 1978

CASE: The Angels receive a message that someone has hired a hit man to kill one of them.

COVERS:
ANGELS: Themselves

FACTS:
First time we see Kelly's 2nd house.
Kelly and Sally Miles are best friends and met at summer camp.

Writer: Edward J. Lakso
Director: Paul Stanley
Producer: Edward J. Lakso

#58— ANGELS IN THE STRETCH
December 20, 1978

CASE: The switching of identical race horses results in the killing of a race track gambler.

COVERS:
Sabrina: Lady jockey
Kelly: Magazine reporter
Kris: Horse buyer from Arizona
Bosley: Horse buyer from Arizona

FASHIONS:
Sabrina is sporting the newest in the lady jockey fashions around the race track!

STAR SIGHTING
David Hedison as Carter Gillis

Writer: Bob Mitchell & Esther Mitchell
Director: Lawrence Doheny
Producer: Edward J. Lakso

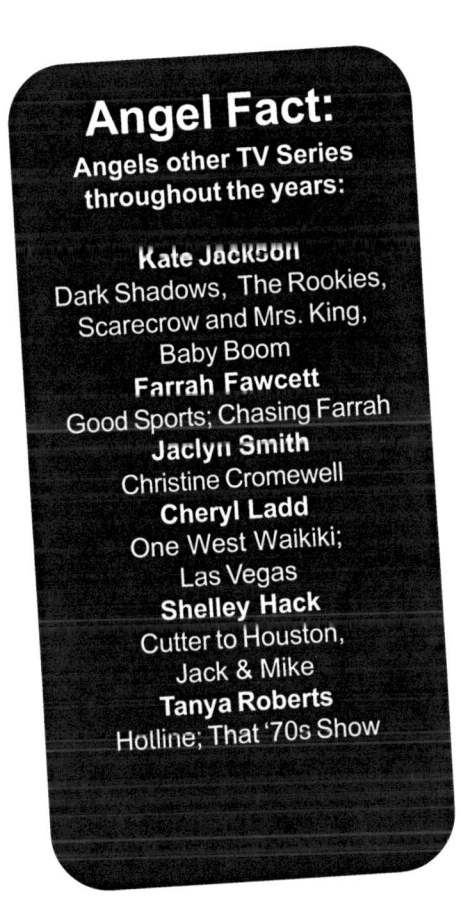

Angel Fact:
Angels other TV Series throughout the years:

Kate Jackson
Dark Shadows, The Rookies, Scarecrow and Mrs. King, Baby Boom
Farrah Fawcett
Good Sports; Chasing Farrah
Jaclyn Smith
Christine Cromewell
Cheryl Ladd
One West Waikiki; Las Vegas
Shelley Hack
Cutter to Houston, Jack & Mike
Tanya Roberts
Hotline; That '70s Show

#59—ANGELS ON VACATION
January 10, 1979

CASE: The Angels go on a vacation to meet Kris's Aunt and Uncle. When they arrive at the small town, all the women seem to be missing and the town's men are not very friendly.

COVERS:
Sabrina: Old woman
Kelly: Old woman
Kris: Old woman

FACTS:
Angels vacation in Arizona.
Kris's CB name is "Sweet Christmas."
Aunt Lydia is the Mayor/Uncle Paul is the Sheriff.
Kris used to hike at "Cave Rock."

FASHIONS:
Sabrina, Kelly & Kris dress up like three Angelic old maids to blend into a crowed of senior citizens.

Writer: Edward J. Lakso
Director: Don Weiss
Producer: Edward J. Lakso

#60 COUNTERFEIT ANGELS
January 24, 1979

CASE: Three female imposters frame the Angels in a rash of robberies.

COVERS:
Sabrina: Sandy Brewster (Carol's sister) pretending to be Sabrina Duncan
Kelly: Pretending to be Kelly Garrett
Kris: Pretending to be Kris Munroe

FACTS:
Charlie is a member of a men's only club.
George Simmons has played golf with Charlie.

FASHIONS:
The biggest difference between real Angels and the imposters were the clothing styles they wore.

TIDBITS:
KBEX, which was a radio station in "Angels on the Air" (#30) is now a TV station in this episode.

Writer: Richard Carr
Director: George Stanford Brown
Producer: Edward J. Lakso

HAVE THE ANGELS TURNED TO CRIME?
Three beautiful Angel look-alikes pull off a series of daring robberies. Now the Angels have to find who's behind the masquerade... before they find themselves behind bars.
CHARLIE'S ANGELS
abc 8:00 PM ③⑤⑧⑨㊵

Brie's Smokin' Cover
"Angel Baby" (#31) Posing as the Millionaires wife, she puffs away throughout the episode.
"The Sandcastle Murders" (#40) Brie lights up while dressed up as a bum.
"Angels Ahoy"(#54) Posing as Sabrina Lampone, she takes a drag in the diner/bar.

TONIGHT, DOUBLE-ACTION

ANGELS SPIN INTO DISCO MURDER!
The Angels make the disco scene to out-hustle a killer who's trying to set a new record for murder.
CHARLIE'S ANGELS
abc 8:00 PM ③ ⑤ ⑧ ⑨ ㊵

#61—DISCO ANGELS
January 21, 1979

CASE: Several elderly men have been strangled near a Disco.

COVERS:
Sabrina: Reporter for a Disco Magazine
Kelly: Saleswoman for "Angelic Records"
Kris: Disco dancer and instructor
Bosley: Himself

FACTS:
Kris dances like her older sister Jill.

SIMILAR EPISODE:
"Little Angels of the Night" (#43)

Writer: George Salvin
Director: Georg Stanford Brown
Producer: Edward J. Lasko

"Angels" on the Walk of Fame

Where in Hollywood would spectators find the greatest stars on television and film under one's feet? Well, it's the Hollywood's very own "Walk of Fame."

Farrah Fawcett's star can be found at 7757 Hollywood Boulevard. A little further down is another angelic star. Jaclyn Smith is at 7000 Hollywood Blvd.

But don't be surprised to hear "Charlie's" voice on the streets of Hollywood. John Forsythe's star is located at 6549 Hollywood Blvd.

The shows' two producers have their own stars. Aaron Spelling's star is located at 6667 Hollywood Blvd and Leonard Goldberg's is at 6901 Hollywood Blvd.

How does one get a star in Hollywood? Easy. First have star power, then donates time to note worthy charities and achieve Entertainment Awards! The Hollywood Star Committee, which is head by top industry individuals, decides who will receive a star each year. Only 20-25 lucky stars receive a star on the "Hollywood Walk of Fame" each year.

#62 - TERROR ON SKIS
(aka: Angels on Skis)
February 7, 1979 2hr movie

CASE: A Government agent is missing. The Angels are called in to protect Carl Hansworth, President's Special advisor to the U.N.

COVERS:
Angels: Bodyguards
Bosley: A drunk

FACTS:
Kelly falls in love with Carl Hansworth.
Sabrina skis the slalom.

STAR SIGHTING:
Dennis Cole as Carl Hansworth

SPECIAL NOTE:
Stock footage from this episode was used in episodes of Spelling/Goldberg's TV series "Vegas" and "Hart of Hart".

Writer: Edward J. Lakso
Director: Don Chaffey
Producer: Edward J. Lakso

#63 - ANGEL IN A BOX
Jill's 3rd return episode
February 14, 1979

CASE: A wealthy man kidnaps Kris to get back at Jill.

COVERS:
Sabrina: French maid
Jill: Jill Johnson
Kelly: Herself
Kris: Herself
Bosley: Johnson Wintergreen

FACTS:
Jill flew in from Montreal.

FASHIONS:
Jill takes off her jacket to show us the "Jill Munroe" we all love.

STAR SIGHTING:
Farrah Fawcett as Jill Munroe
John Colicos as Anton Karazna

Writer: Curtis Harrington
Director: Edward J. Lakso
Producer: Edward. J. Lakso

Lovestories
Season Three

Angels in Vegas (episode #47)
Sabrina once again falls for the Angels client. This time it was the owner of the Tropicana, Frank Howell (Dean Martin). Even this Angel could not get the gambler away from the craps tables.

Angel Come Home (episode #48)
Jill becomes engaged to be married, to the sexy Steve Cormody (Steven Collins). Before the two can become one, Cormody is killed when he test drives Jill's car. Cormody goes to heaven as Jill sheds tears.

Angels on High (episode #49)
Kelly starts having feelings for the soon to be wealthy Bill Freedman. Not even Kelly was enough to keep Freedman's free spirit on Earth.

Terror on Skis (episode #62)
Kelly is protecting the handsome government agent Carl Hansworth (Dennis Cole), but after a political terrorist is captured, politics wins back Hansworth's heart.

ANOTHER GREAT WEDNESDAY NIGHT ON ABC!
KRIS KIDNAPPED! IS SHE BAIT FOR A BIGGER CATCH?
Farrah Fawcett-Majors guest stars!
CHARLIE'S ANGELS
abc 9:00 PM 7 ⑪ ⑬

#65—MARATHON ANGELS
March 7, 1979

CASE: The daughter of an oil-rich Arab is in danger of being kidnapped during a marathon run.

COVERS:
Sabrina: Herself
Kelly: Runner
Kris: Runner

FASHIONS:
Kris and Kelly running the streets of LA in very small running outfits. Let's get physical.

TIDBITS:
The Angels run though the 20th Century Fox studio where "Charlie's Angels" was filmed.

STAR SIGHTING:
Sarah Purcell as Millicent Krail

Writer: Edward J. Lakso
Director: Bob Kelljan
Producer: Edward J. Lakso

#64 - TEEN ANGELS
February 28, 1979

CASE: A group of spoiled rich girls are being blackmailed to sell drugs & liquor at a girls school.

COVERS:
Sabrina: Art teacher
Kelly: English teacher
Kris: Student
Bosley: Groomer in stables

FACTS:
The Angels become honoree graduates of "Blackmoor" College,
Bosley can drive a tractor.
Angels get a vacation to Acapulco from the Charlie.

FASHIONS
Kris, Kelly & Sabrina all walking around the campus in their gorgeous nightgowns. What a campus!

TIDBITS:
The school used for Blackmoor College was also used in the 1975 film "Satan's School for Girls" which starred Kate Jackson & Cheryl Ladd.

STAR SIGHTING:
Audrey Landers as Donna

Writer: Bob Mitchell and Esther Mitchell
Story by: Laurie Lakso
Director: Allen Baron
Producer: Edward J. Lakso

GIRL'S CAMPUS TERRORIZED BY KILLER...ANGELS ENROLL TO STOP HIM!
Death strikes an exclusive girls school...and the Angels hit the campus for a crash course in murder!
CHARLIE'S ANGELS
ⓐⓑⓒ 8:00PM ③⑤⑧⑨㊵

Season Three Opening Sequence   (1978-1979)

1. Police Academy Shot
2. Sabrina at police firing range
3. Kelly in police defense class
4. Kris S.F.P.D. driver training
5. Sabrina a police parking attendant
6. Kelly a police crosswalk guard
7. Kris on the police phone switch board
8. Sabrina & Kelly walking out of Police Department and Kris joins them
9. Silhouette Angel with Walkie-Talkie and lettering "Kate Jackson"
10. Race Car Driving - Episode "Hellride"
11. Sabrina jumping onto pole - Episode "Mother Angel"
12. Sabrina squatting - Episode "Pilot Film"
13. Sabrina at the office bar - Episode "Angels in Paradise"
14. Sabrina clapping her hands - Episode "Angels in Paradise"
15. Silhouette Angel with Gun and lettering "Jaclyn Smith"
16. Kelly running from her car - Episode "Angels on Wheels"
17. Kelly on motor cycle - Episode "Pilot Film"
18. Kelly taking a photo with camera - Episode "The Killing Kind"
19. Kelly doing a turn and putting on a hat - Episode "Night of the Strangler"
20. Kelly with head over shoulder - Episode "The Killing Kind"
21. Silhouette Angel with Gun and lettering "Cheryl Ladd"
22. Kris is running in blue jump suit - (unknown episode)
23. Kris in a magic show - Episode "Pretty Angels All in a Row"
24. Kris on boat in bathing suit - Episode "Angels in Paradise"
25. Kris having knives thrown at her - Episode "Circus of Terror"
26. Kris in a hot tub - Episode "Angel in Love"
27. Silhouette of Bosley and lettering "David Doyle"
28. Bosley handing a gift - Episode "Hellride"
29. Bosley riding golf cart - Episode "Angels in Vegas"
30. Charlie's Angles Logo and Exploding

#66—ANGELS IN WAITING
March 21, 1979

CASE: Bosley is fed up being predictable so he plays a game of "cat & mouse" with the Angels.

COVERS:
ANGLES: Themselves

FACTS:
Bosley eats at "The Chelsea" restaurant every day.
Bosley's license plate is CA 950WUJ.
Bosley is going to the Bahamas for vacation.

FASHIONS:
The Angels have no time to get into their bathing suits doing all Bosley's paperwork at the office.

STAR SIGHTING:
Pat Crowley as Ellen

Writer: Edward J. Lakso
Director: Allen Baron
Producer: Edward J. Lakso

#67—ROSEMARY FOR REMEMBRANCE
(aka: An Angel Called Rosemary)
May 2, 1979

CASE: An ex-gangster recently released from prison is the target for a killer.

COVERS:
Sabrina: Writer of a Prohibition Book
Kelly: Herself
Kris: "Rosemary"/Herself
Bosley: Mob Associate

FACTS:
Kris's photo is seen in "The McCully Fraud" newspaper.
Kris dances a mean Charleston.

FASHIONS:
Kris looks elegant in those 30's dresses. It just goes to show you an Angel can be in any era and still look heavenly.

STAR SIGHTING:
Ramon Bieri as Jake Garfield

Writer: Lee Sheldon
Director: Ronald Austin
Producers: Ronald Austin & James Buchanan

#68—ANGELS REMEMBERED
Final Episode of the 3rd season
Sabrina's Last Case
(aka: Angels Revisited)
May 16, 1979

CASE: Charlie throws a party for his Angels to thank them for three years of service (two for Kris). The Angels drink champagne, eat cake and highlight their past cases. Notable cases are: *Angels in Paradise; Angels on Ice; Angels in Vegas; Circus of Terror* and *Antique Angels*.

COVERS:
Various

FACTS:
Kelly will vacation in New York.
Kris will vacation in Bimini.
Sabrina will vacation in Rome.
Bosley had three pieces of cake.
Kris's Birthday was last month.

SIMILAR EPISODE:
#109 Let Our Angel Live

FASHIONS:
Kelly remembers that outstanding belly dancing she did in "Angels on Ice" (#24). Like anyone had forgotten! Dance on and on!

Written: Edward J. Lakso
Director: Kim Manners
Producer: Edward J. Lakso

Angels Fact:
Charlie's Angels was filmed on Sound Stage #8 on The 20th Century Fox

The *Cheryl Ladd* Scrapbook

Here are some personal photos from my days on the set of "Charlie's Angels"! I hope you get a kick out these photos. ~ Cheryl

On the set of "Rosemary For Remembrance" with my hair stylist Norma Lee for all 4 years on Charlie's Angels

Angel WRAP Party 1978!

Celebrating the completion of my first season on Charlie's Angels with Kate, Jackie, and producers Leonard Goldberg & Aaron Spelling

David saying a few words as we looked on with a little girl named Tori Spelling!!

My "real life" Angel, Jordan on the set of "Terror on Skis."

Just having a good time with Shelley Hack while filming "Love Boat Angels."

This was Shelley's first episode. What a fun time we had!

My brother Seth came by the set to meet "ALL" the Angels including Farrah!

On the set in my "little Bo Peep" outfit from "Angels Ahoy."

Taking a break with Jackie and the director, Don Chaffey.

A very cold day of filming on "Terror on Skis"

Having fun on the set in St. Barts with Shelley, Bert Convy and Bo Hopkins while we filmed "Love Boat Angels"

My mother, Dolores sitting at Bosley's desk on the set of "Angels Remembered".

Two Classy Cats...on the set of "Love Boat Angels" with director Kim Manners.

Horsing around with David when taking a break while filming "Love Boat Angels" I miss him so.....

Celebrating my Birthday on the set of "Angel Come Home"

Season Four

Angels:
Kelly Garrett (Jaclyn Smith)
Kris Munroe (Cheryl Ladd)
Tiffany Welles (Shelley Hack)
Jill Munroe (Farrah Fawcett)

Airing: ABC, Wednesdays 9pm - 10pm

Angel Season Run:
September 13 1979- May 16, 1980

Angel Season Rating:
#20 - 20.9 audience

Angel Episode Estimated Cost:
$450,000

Angel Opener:
Once Upon a Time...there were three little girls who went to the police academy... one in Los Angeles...one in San Francisco..the other in Boston.. and they each were assigned very hazardous duties...but I took them away from all that and now they work for me..my name is Charlie.

Angel Awards: Golden Globe Nominated:
David Doyle for "Best Supporting Actor in a Series, Mini-series, or Motion Picture made for TV" (1980)

Missing Angel: Sabrina Duncan left the Agency to get married which included children in her Angelic future.

Angel Changes:
Sabrina ran off and got married. She left the Angels and made Charlie search for a new girl. He found Tiffany Welles, a tall, smart, good-looking replacement. Although Tiffany brought an elegance to the show, she did not have the audience draw like her former Angel.

Angel Clothing Change: The Angels took the high road to "High Fashion" when Tiffany Welles walked into the office.

#69—LOVE BOAT ANGELS
(*aka Angels In The Sun*)
September 9, 1979 - 2hr premier
Tiffany Welles first case

CASE: $5 million worth of museum antiques are stolen. The Angels track down the thieves who plan to sell off the pieces and give the profits to free people in the Middle East.

COVERS:
Kelly: Herself
Kris: A high roller thief
Tiffany: Herself
Bosley: Buyer of fenced antiques

FACTS:
Sabrina is married and is pregnant.
Charlie is old friends with Tiffany's father.
Tiffany's father is head of the detectives in Boston and her mother teaches Latin.
Townsend Agency's new linen service is "STAR".
Angels meet "The Love Boat" cast.

FASHIONS:
Angels are found in their new bathing suits around "The Love Boat" pool. Gopher, Doc & Issac are in love!!

STAR SIGHTING:
"The Love Boat" cast
Bert Convy as Paul Hollister
Bo Hopkins as Wes Anderson
Dick Sargent as James Avery
Judy Landers as Blond Girl

Writer: Edward J. Lakso
Director: Allen Baron
Producer: Edward J. Lakso

Angel Fact:
The main title music was written by Jack Elliot & Allyn Ferguson

#70—ANGELS GO TRUCKIN'
(aka: Angel Trucker)
September 19, 1979

CASE: The Venus trucking company has lost a million dollar shipment of pharmaceuticals.

COVERS:
Kelly: Waitress
Kris: Trucker/"Angel Eyes"
Tiffany: Trucker
Bosley: Himself

FACTS:
Kris knows Pig Latin.
Charlie owns the "Venus" trucking company.
Tiffany & Kris graduate from a trucking school.

FASHIONS:
Kris a.k.a. "Angel Eyes" has every man on the CB band imaging her in a bikini! Copy that!

Director: Richard Carr
Writer: Lawrence Dobkin
Producer: Robert Janes

#71—AVENGING ANGEL
September 26, 1979

CASE: Desmond, an ex-heroine addict is released from prison and plans to seek revenge on Kelly.

COVERS:
Angels: Themselves

FACTS:
Kelly eats frequently at a restaurant called "Guido's."
Kelly was an undercover officer four years ago/

STAR SIGHTING:
Cameron Mitchell as Frank Desmond

Writer: Edward J. Lakso
Story By: Laurie Lakso
Director: Allen Barron
Producer: Edward J. Lakso

#72—ANGELS AT THE ALTAR
October 3, 1979

CASE: Kelly's friend is getting married, but someone wants the groom dead.

COVERS:
Kelly: Herself
Kris: Maid
Tiffany: Violinist
Bosley: Bartender

FACTS:
Kelly and Sharon are old friends.
Kelly got sick at Sharon's 18th birthday.
Tiffany can play a mean violin.

STAR SIGHTING:
Kim Cattrall as Sharon
John David Carson as Scott Miller
Adrienne Larussa as Claudia
Marie Windsor as Gloria Kellerman

Writer: Larry Alexander
Director: Lawrence Dobkin
Producer: Robert Janes

#73—FALLEN ANGEL
October 24, 1979
Jill's fourth episode

CASE: The Angels are hired to protect the "Blue Heron Diamond" from the jewel thief Damien Roth.

COVERS:
Jill: Damion Roth's girlfriend/thief
Kelly: Allison Beckworth, a writer
Tiffany: A car buff
Kris: Herself

FACTS:
Jill has won the Grand Prix.
Charlie knew the clients father.

FASHIONS:
Jill still has not found a bra! You would think after winning the Grand Prix she could afford one!

STAR SIGHTING:
Farrah Fawcett as Jill Munroe
Timothy Dalton as Damien Roth

TIDBITS:
This is the only episode where an Angel worked undercover without the other Angels knowing. Jill Munroe is undercover as the girlfriend to Damien Roth and is thought to have turned to a life of crime.

Writer: Kathryn Michaelian Powers
Director: Allen Baron
Producer: Robert Janes

#74—CAGED ANGEL
October 31, 1979

CASE: A young woman prisoner is killed during a jewel heist.

COVERS:
Kelly: Sister Theresa
Kris: Kristine Martin #5270
Tiffany: Sister Mary

FACTS:
Charlie sets up a trust fund for the deceased woman's son.

SIMILAR EPISODE:
#4 "Angels in Chains"

FASHIONS:
Kris is striped naked, sprayed and searched just like her fellow Angels three years ago.

STAR SIGHTING:
Sally Kirkland as Lonnie
Shirley Stoler as Big Aggie

Writer: B.W. Sandefur
Director: Dennis Donnelly
Producer: Elaine Rich

Angel Fact:
In the series Charlie Townsend owned another business! An all woman trucking company, called Venus Trucking!
Episode: Angels Go Truckin' #70

#75—ANGELS ON THE STREET
November 7, 1979

CASE: A dance instructor is brutally beaten for no apparent reason.

COVERS:
Kelly: Hooker
Kris: Herself
Tiffany: Hooker

FASHIONS:
Tiffany and Kelly looking good in their tight silk pants! A thousand dollars? That's cheap even for Angels!

Writer: Edward J. Lakso
Director: Don Chaffey
Producer: Edward J. Lakso

Memorable Kris Moments
Circus of Terror (#27)
Knives being thrown at Kris.
Angels in Paradise (#23)
A palm tree branch covering Kris's naked body
Angel Baby (#31)
First time Kris shoots a man with a gun
Angels in the Wings (#32)
Kris sings on a film set.
Winning is for Losers (#51)
Kris wrestles an alligator

#76—THE PRINCE AND THE ANGEL
November 14 1979 - Jill's fifth episode

CASE: A Prince has taken refuge in Los Angeles from an assassination attempt and falls in love with Jill Munroe.

COVERS:
Themselves

FACTS:
Angels throw a Birthday party for Charlie.
Kelly buys a purple sweater and Jill buys a tie for Charlie's Birthday.

FASHIONS:
Jill still does her best work in a tube top!

STAR SIGHTING:
Farrah Fawcett as Jill Munroe

Writer: Edward J. Lakso
Story by: Laurie Lakso
Director: Cliff Bole
Producer: Edward J. Lakso

Jill's affair with a playboy prince becomes a flirtation with death!
Special guest: Farrah Fawcett
CHARLIE'S ANGELS
abc 8:00PM ③⑤⑧⑨㊵

A SMASHING NIGHT!

#77—ANGELS ON SKATES
November 21, 1979

CASE: The Angels skate into a case of a kidnapped skater with a million dollar ransom for her return.

COVERS:
Kelly: Tara White, "Roller Disco" magazine
Kris: Professional skater
Tiffany: Yvonne Henning, "Roller Disco" magazine
Bosley: Orwen Redbert, West Cost Roller Derby

FACTS:
The Angels take skating lessons at Venice Beach.

FASHIONS:
Kris looks like the speed of light in her red hot silk pants! You go Angel!

STAR SIGHTING:
Rene Auberjonois as Freddie Fortune
Ed Begley Jr. as Kenny
Virgil Frye as Otis

Writer: Michael Michalian & John Francis Whelpley?
Director: Don Chaffey
Producer: Robert Janes

#78—ANGELS ON CAMPUS
November 28, 1979

CASE: After young women are missing from Tiffany's almamater, the Angels uncover that a charming English professor is kidnapping and selling college girls into white slavery.

COVERS:
Kelly: Football drafter
Kris: Student
Tiffany: Big sister/freelance writer
Bosley: Football drafter

FACTS:
Tiffany was President of Kappa Omega PSI.
Tiffany attended Whitley College.

FASHIONS:
Tiffany finds herself changing out of a towel and finds darts shooting at her.

Writer: Michael Michaelian
Director: Don Chaffey
Producer: Robert Janes & Elain Rich

Season Four Opening Sequence (1979-1980)

1. Police Academy Shot
2. Kelly in police defense class
3. Kris S.F.P.D. driver training
4. Tiffany is on police shooting range
5. Kelly a police crosswalk guard
6. Kris on the police phone switch board
7. Tiffany doing Police paper work
8. Kelly walking out of Police Department and Kris & Tiffany joins her
9. Silhouette Angel with Gun and lettering "Jaclyn Smith"
10. Kelly running from her car - Episode "Angels on Wheels"
11. Kelly on motor cycle - Episode "Pilot Film"
12. Kelly taking a photo with camera - Episode "The Killing Kind"
13. Kelly doing a turn and putting on a hat - Episode "Night of the Strangler"
14. Kelly with head over shoulder Episode "The Killing Kind"
15. Silhouette Angel with Gun and lettering "Cheryl Ladd"
16. Kris is running in blue jump suit - (unknown episode)
17. Kris in a magic show - Episode "Pretty Angels All in a Row"
18. Kris on boat in bathing suit - Episode "Angels in Paradise"
19. Kris having knives thrown at her - Episode "Circus of Terror"
20. Kris in a hot tub - Episode "Angel in Love"
21. Silhouette Angel with Walkie-Talkie and lettering "Shelley Hack"
22. Tiffany running - Episode "Angel Hunt"
23. Tiffany on a speed boat -Episode "Love Boat Angels"
24. Tiffany in a white suit - Episode "Love Boat Angels'
25. Tiffany driving a truck - Episode "Angels Go Trucking"
26. Tiffany at the office bar - Episode "Angels on Campus"
    alternate - Tiffany in office in white shirt/blue jacket - Episode "Angels at the Alter"
27. Silhouette of Bosley and lettering "David Doyle"
28. Bosley handing a gift - Episode "Hellride"
29. Bosley riding golf cart - Episode "Angels in Vegas"
30. Charlie's Angles Logo and Exploding

#79—ANGEL HUNT
December 5, 1979

CASE: Kris mistakes a voice on the phone for Charlie's. The Angels then fly to Mazatlan thinking they are going to help Charlie but find themselves the bait to lure Charlie to a killer.

COVERS:
Themselves

FACTS:
Tiffany is learning to surf.
Kris is a real "Tarzan" fan.

SIMILAR EPISODES:
#5 Target: Angels

FASHIONS:
Kris and Kelly are gracing two new bathing suits as they show Tiffany how to surf. They are real beach bunnies!

Writer: Lee Sheldon
Director: Paul Stanley
Producer: Robert Janes

#80—CRUISING ANGELS
(aka: The Wayward Angels)
December 12, 1979

CASE: The Angels find $7 million worth of stolen gold bars on Charlie's new yacht after it was discovered missing for an evening.

COVERS:
Angels: Themselves
Bosley: Dr. Bosley

FACTS:
Kris hates champagne.
Charlie is on business in Paris.
"Wayward Angel" is 1000, foot yacht.

FASHIONS:
Everyone is clothed but Bosley did lose the "Wayward Angel"! Good job, Boz.

STAR SIGHTING:
Beverly Garland as Pat Justice

Writer: B.W. Sandefur
Director: George McCowan
Producer: Robert Janes & Elaine Rich

Angel Facts
Some of the Angels had nicknames for each other on the series!
Sabrina: Brie
Kelly: Kel
Tiffany: Tiff
Bosley: Boz

#82—ANGEL'S CHILD
January 9, 1980

CASE: Kelly takes an abused child under her wings and helps the boy's father seek help to.

COVERS:
Themselves

FACTS:
Kelly's second house is seen.

The Angels must turn on their answering machines when they leave the house. And turn them off as soon as they get home.

Writer: Edward J. Lakso
Director: Dennis Donnelly
Producer: Edward J. Lakso

#81—OF GHOSTS & ANGELS
(aka: Ghosts and Goblins and Angels)
January 1, 1980

CASE: Tiffany's nightmares comes true after she visits her wealthy college friend.

COVERS:
Themselves

FACTS:
Tiffany has physic powers and she worked with Dr. Kempler a famous ghost hunter.
Tiffany and Erica are college friends and were known as "Terrors of Tracy Hall."

FASHIONS:
Tiffany wakes up at 2:30am in full make up and an elegant nightgown from a nightmare. How about some warm milk?

STAR SIGHTING:
Robin Mattson as Erica

Written: Kathryan Michaelian Powers
Director: Cliff Bole
Producer: Robert James

#83—ONE OF OUR ANGELS ARE MISSING
January 16, 1980

CASE: When a jewel thief/rapist skips town after killing a man, Kris goes undercover as a wealthy divorcee to bring him back to Los Angeles.

COVERS:
Kelly: Realtor
Kris: A wealthy divorcee
Tiffany: Mrs. Stevens, a house buyer
Bosley: Security and electronic man

FACTS:
Charlie gives Kris an expensive bracelet for a great job well done.

FASHIONS:
Kris is really the bait in a two piece swim suit. The fish will surely bite!

Writer: Robert S. Bihenller and W. Dal Jenkins
Director: Allen Baron
Producer: Edward J. Lakso

#84—CATCH A FALLING ANGEL
January 23, 198

CASE: A reported missing person leads the Angels into the world of pornography to find a killer.

COVERS:
Kelly: Herself
Kris: Porno actress
Tiffany: Herself

FASHIONS:
Kris is very HOT in her tight pink pants. She really shapes into the part well.

Writer: Edward J. Lakso
Director: Kim Manners
Producer: Edward J. Lakso

Kelly's Car Problems

Kelly seems to have no luck with cars. Regardless of the danger to her, Bosley was never happy to replace her vehicle.

Kelly's Car Explosions!
Angels on Wheels (#12);
Toni's Boys (#91)

Kelly's Brakes Give-Out!
Angels on Wheels (#12)
One Love, Two Angels (#92-93)
Taxi Angels (#102)

Kelly Gets Rammed Off The Road!
Angels on the Air (#30)
Moonshinin' Angels (#100)

#85—HOMES, $WEET HOMES
January 30, 1980

CASE: A wealthy couples mansion is robbed during an open house.

COVERS:
Kelly: Ms. Doolittle from Pepsi Cola
Kris: Real estate agent
Tiffany: Ms. Tiffany Ludlow
Bosley: Jake Pickins, buyer of letters

FACTS:
Albert Smith is spotted in this episode and Kelly feeds him from a fork

FASHIONS:
Kris defends herself in a two piece swim suit. Karate chops never looked better!

Written: William Froug
Story By: William Froug, Robert Lee, Ronald E. Osborne
Director: Alen Barron
Producer: Elaine Rich

#86—DANCIN' ANGELS
February 6, 1980

CASE: At a 1930s themed dance contest a female contestant disappears.

COVERS:
Kelly: Dancer
Kris: Dancer
Tiffany: Dancer/Bosley's partner
Bosley: Dancer/Talent agent

FACTS:
Tiffany and Bosley dance a mean tango on the dance floor.

FASHIONS:
Once again the Angels look smashing in any period clothing! The '30s never looked so good.

STAR SIGHTING:
Caesar Romero as Elton Mills
Norman Alden as P.J. Wilkes
Brad Maule as Joe Fairgate

Writer: Edward J. Lakso
Director: Dennis Donnelly
Producer: Edward J. Lakso

Employee Angel Card: Tiffany Welles

Born: Boston, Mass

Family: Father head of Boston Police Dept. Detectives

Schooling: Whitley College — head of Kappa Omega PSI 1979 -Graduated from the Boston Police Academy.

Address: Owns a home in Los Angeles. (Is the same house Darrin & Samantha Stephens' lived in on **Bewitched**)

Employment: Townsend Detective Agency, Los Angeles 1979-1980

Nickname: Tiff

Pets: None

Boyfriends: None

Marriage: Single

Best Friends: Kelly Garrett, Kris Munroe, Bosley; Erica Burke (#81) - old college friend

Car: Ford Pinto - Orange/Red - company car (originally was Sabrina Ducan's car)

Interests: Playing violin, baking cookies, nurses aide, physic powers

Best Detective Skills: Quick thinking — excellent driver

Angelic Heaven

Angel's kidnapper has love in his heart and murder on his mind!

Charlie's Angels

GUEST STAR: FARRAH FAWCETT

abc 9:00PM ②⑤⑨

#87—HARRIGAN'S ANGELS
February 20, 1980

CASE: The Angels are hired to help detective Harry Harrigan find missing micro-electronics. The Angels' uncover that their client is the thief.

COVERS:
Themselves

FACTS:
Kris's father was an alcoholic and she can't cook. Tiffany bakes cookies and the Angels are very fond of dairy products.

Writer: Edward J. Lakso
Director: Don Chaffey
Producer: Edward J. Lakso

#89—NIPS AND TUCKS
March 5, 1980

CASE: A well known criminal is trying to change his identity at a prestigious plastic surgery clinic.

COVERS:
Kelly: Paramedics
Kris: Paramedics
Tiffany: Nurse
Bosley: Patient

FACTS:
Tiffany was a nurses aide in college.
Tiffany's cousin had plastic surgery after a tragic automobile accident.

FASHIONS:
The Angels are looking Angelic in scrubs.

Writer: B.W. Sandefur
Story by: B.W. Sandefur & Cory Applebaum
Director: Don Chaffey
Producer: Elaine Rich

#88—AN ANGEL'S TRAIL
Jill's final episode
February 27, 1980

CASE: Jill Munroe is kidnapped after witnessing a robbery at a gas station.

COVERS:
Themselves

FACTS:
Jill was on her way to visit a little girl with Leukemia.
Jill bakes a mean chocolate cake.

TIDBITS:
Farrah Fawcett's final episode.
Farrah only has one scene with Cheryl & David in this episode.
Episode plot is similar to the John Stienbeck's novel "Of Mice and Men"

STAR SIGHTING:
Farrah Fawcett as Jill Munroe

Writer: Wayne Cruseturner
Director: Dennis Donnelly
Producer: Robert Janes

Angel Fact:
Charlie's Angels ran for five seasons! But Farrah Fawcett was only on the first season! Fawcett came back for six guest episodes during 1978-1980 seasons!

> Daring ring of thieves plans deadly new job: put the Angels out of business... for keeps!
>
> **Charlie's Angels**
> Special Time!
> abc 8:00PM ⑦⑧

#90—THREE FOR THE MONEY
March, 12 1980

CASE: The Angels set a three prong attack on a con artist.

COVERS:
Kelly: Streetwise Girl
Kris: Wealthy Lady
Tiffany: Senators Aid
Bosley: Dr. Olgberg

SIMILAR EPISODE:
#14 The Big Tap Out

Writer: Lee Sheldon
Director: George McCowan
Producer: Edward J. Lakso

Angel Fact:

Shelley Hack was a high fashion model before becoming an Angel!

#91—TONI'S BOYS
April 2, 1980

CASE: A recently paroled prisoner wants the Angels dead. Charlie hires his good friend Antonia Blake and her male detectives to protect his Angels.

ANGELS & TONI'S BOYS COVERS
Kelly: Herself
Kris: Singer
Tiffany: Model

Cotton: Horse expert
Matt: Drummer/Stripper
Bob: Model

FACTS:
Tiffany has a birthday.
Tiffany lives in the same house that Darrin & Samantha Stephens lived in on the TV Series, **Bewitched.**
Bosley is on a trip.
Kelly's car blows up again for the second time in the series, first time it blew up was in "Angels on Wheels" (#12).

FASHIONS:
Having male Angels, Matt's the one
who takes off his shirt! You go boy!

STAR SIGHTING:
Robert Loggia as Michael Durano
Barbara Stanwyck as Antonia Blake

TIDBITS:
This episode re-enacts a classic scene from Edgar Allan Poe's "The Cask of Amontillado" when the badguys seal up the Angels in the wine cellar.
Toni's Boys was to be a **Charlie's Angels** spin-off series for **ABC**. Yet the series was never picked up.

Writer: Katharyn Powers
Director: Ron Satlof
Producer: Robert Janes

#92 & #93—ONE LOVE..TWO ANGELS
(aka: Angel in Love)
2 part episode
Tiffany's last case
April 30 & May 7, 1980

CASE: Kelly finds out she is the daughter of a millionaire. After a tearful reunion, her "father" dies of a heart attack. Kelly hires the Angels to find out who she really is.

COVERS:
Themselves
Tiffany: A reporter

FACTS:
Tiffany recently bought an Encyclopedia set.
Kelly as a child lived at the St. Agnes Orphanage in Texas.
Kelly as a child lived in foster homes.
"The Plains" - foster family brought Kelly to Los Angeles.
Kris and Kelly lost their friendship & resign from the agency after they both fall in love with the same man. But these Angels make up and rip up their resignations
This was Tiffany Welles final case.

TIDBIT:
This is the only episode that originally aired in two parts.

STAR SIGHTING:
Patrick Duffy as Bill Cord
Robert Reed as Glen Staley

Writer: B.W. Sandefur
Director: Dennis Donnelly
Producer: Elaine Rich

Kris and Kelly in Love Feud Over the Same Man!
Special Guest: Patrick ("Dallas") Duffy
Charlie's Angels
9:00PM

Tiffany's best Non-Detective Skills
*Plays Violin *Speaks Fluent French
*Physic Powers *Bakes Cookies *Nurses
Aid* A Ghost Hunter *Expert Tango Dancer

Lovestories
Season Four

Love Boat Angels
(episode #69)
Kris is a real sucker for the bad guy as she finds herself falling for Paul Hollister (Bert Convy), who is a modern day Robin Hood. But oil and water don't mix. Kris sails way.

Fallen Angel (episode #73)
Jill goes deep undercover to find her heart in tangles with a jewel thief, Damien Roth (Timothy Dalton). Even her 007 role hurts when Jill sends Roth to the big house as she holds onto the diamond.

The Prince and the Angel
(episode #76)
Princess Jill? Once upon a time...Jill meets Prince Eric and falls in love. The Angels must keep an eye out on this royal couple to keep both in safety. But all fairy tales end and so did the love affair.

Cruising Angels (episode #80)
Aboard Charlie's "Wayward Angel" ship, Bosley finds himself shipwrecked with the lovely Pat Justice. This decorator is more into gold smuggling than snuggling up to Bosley.

One Love, Two Angels
(episode #92-93)
Kris and Kelly find themselves in love with the same man, Bill Cord (Patrick Duffy). Bill feels he found his sole mates in these two Angels. Only Bill's death can mend the Angel friendship and find his killer.

Season Five

Angels:
Kelly Garrett (Jaclyn Smith)
Kris Munroe (Cheryl Ladd)
Julie Rogers (Tanya Roberts)

Angel Airing:
Sundays 8pm - 9pm
Saturdays 8pm - 9pm

Angel Season Run:
Sundays: November 16, 1980- January 11, 1981
Saturdays: January 24, 1981 - February 28, 1981
Wednesdays: June 3, 1981-June 24, 1981

Angel Season Rating:
#47

Angel Episode Estimated Cost:
$650,000

Angel Opening:
Once Upon a time there were three beautiful girls...two of them graduated from the police academy...the other graduated from a top school for models..they each reaped the awards of their exciting careers...but, I took them away from all that and now they work for me...my name is Charlie.

Angel Missing:
It was a fast year for Tiffany, as she decided to stay back east for a while. Julie Rogers, the new Angel, was a model-turned -detective and then joined the Townsend agency. The Angels left Los Angeles for the sunny islands of Hawaii, where their heavenly bodies were found in bikinis every second of their stay. Even the hot bathing suits could not stop these Angels from finally getting their pink slips.

Angel Changes: The Angels lost the classy-elegant clothing and found themselves in Hawaii walking around in bathing suits once again!

#94—ANGEL IN HIDING
November 30, 1980
First 2 Hours of the premiere
Julie Rogers first case

CASE: After a fashion model is murdered, the Angels go undercover into the shady world of modeling.

COVERS:
Kelly: Model/friend of the dead girl
Kris: Model
Julie: Model/dead girl's roommate

FACTS:
Kelly takes cream in her coffee.
The reason for Tiffany being absent from the office was simply explained that she has decided to stay back east for awhile.
Julie's background: Julie was born in New York City, where her father left her mother and then she died. She was caught shoplifting at age 14 and spent 6 months in a correctional center. Now she's a fashion model turned semi-detective by friend and parole officer Harry Stearns.

FASHIONS:
New Angel Julie is found in her first "Angel" bathing suit! First episode that all 3 Angels appear together in swimsuits

STAR SIGHTING:
Vic Morrow as Harry Stearns
Jack Albertson as Edward Jordan

TIDBITS:
The original airing was a three hour premiere episode on the Angels new night, Sundays. The episode was originally titled "Street Models to Hawaiian Angels." Later the episode was split into three part for syndication and re-titled "Angels in Hiding" (part 1 &2) & "To See An Angel Die."

Writer: Edward J. Lakso
Director: Dennis Donnelly
Producer: Edward J. Lakso

#95-TO SEE AN ANGEL DIE
Third hour of the premiere
First Hawaiian episode
November 30, 1980

CASE: A man seeks revenge on Kris for the death of his wife.

COVERS:
Themselves

FACTS:
The nameplate for the Townsend Agency shows that Charlie has offices in Los Angeles, Paris & Hawaii. The office address is 4376 Kahaii Ave. The book "Hansel and Gretal" is Kris's good luck charm.
Kris's full name is: Kristine Munroe.
Kris's car in Hawaii is a Black Chevrolet Convertible, with the license number #7F-88441.

FASHIONS:
With the Angels in Hawaii out come the bathing suits! Why do you think they are on the islands?? For the snow? Think again.

TIDBIT:
The Townsend Agency office in Hawaii was Leilani Sako's office home in "Angels in Paradise" (# 23).

STAR SIGHTING:
Jane Wyman as Eleanor Willard
Soon-Teck Oh as Lt. Torre

Written by: Edward J. Lakso
Director: Dennis Donnelly
Producer: Edward J. Lakso

Lovestories

Season Five

Angel on a Roll (episode #107)
Kris needs to have the dashing Ted Markham spend some of his stolen money in order to establish the fact he is a thief. Too bad crime doesn't pay!

#96—ANGELS OF THE DEEP
(aka: Diamond Head Angels)
Second Hawaii episode
December 7, 1980

CASE: Julie and her new friend are terrorized while scuba diving.

COVERS:
Themselves

FACTS:
Julie's Hawaiian car is a Yellow Jeep.
Julie learned how to scuba dive.
Bosley losses all his important papers in the pool.

FASHIONS:
The sea in Hawaii never looked more beautiful with both Julie and Kris in their scuba gear! Sunken treasure? Where?

STAR SIGHTING:
Patti D'Arbanville as Bianca Blake
Sonny Bono as Walrus
Anne Francis as Cindy Lee

Written: Robert George
Director: Kim Manners
Producer: Robert Janes

Season Five Opening Sequence (1980-1981)

1. Police Academy Shot
2. Kelly in police defense class
3. Kris S.F.P.D. driver training
4. Julie graduating from Modeling School
5. Kelly a police crosswalk guard
6. Kris on the police phone switch board
7. Julie on a photo shoot for "Joggerade"
8. Kelly walking out of Police Department and Kris & Julie joins her
9. Silhouette Angel with Gun and lettering "Jaclyn Smith"
10. Kelly in chorus line - Episode "Angels in Vegas"
11. Kelly doing a turn and putting on a hat - Episode "Night of the Strangler"
12. Kelly with head over shoulder - Episode "The Killing Kind"
13. Kelly in a blue jumpsuit- Episode "From Hawaiian Angels to Street Models"
    alternate - Kelly in Southern Belle Outfit - Episode "Of Ghosts and Angels"
14. Kelly in a red blouse on office couch - Episode "Taxi Angels"
    alternate - Kelly in blue flowered top- Episode "Hula Angels"
15. Silhouette Angel with Gun and lettering "Cheryl Ladd"
16. Kris with pom, poms - Episode "Pom Pom Angles"
17. Kris in a magic show - Episode "Pretty Angels All in a Row"
18. Kris on boat in bathing suit - Episode "Angels in Paradise"
19. Kris having knives thrown at her - Episode "Circus of Terror"
20. Kris in a hot tub - Episode "Angel in Love"
21. Silhouette Angel with Walkie-Talkie and lettering "Tanya Roberts"
22. Julie holding a gun - Episode "Angels of the Deep"
23. Julie running on beach in a blue/white bikini - (unknown episode)
24. Julie on top of speeding car - Episode "From Hawaiian Angels to Street Models"
25. Julie all wet in a bathing suit "Waikiki Angels"
26. Julie with a red flower in her hair - Episode "Island Angels"
27. Silhouette of Bosley and lettering "David Doyle"
28. Bosley handing a gift - Episode "Hellride"
29. Bosley falling into office pool - Episode "Angels of the Deep"
    alternate - Bosley floating in office pool - Episode "Angels of the Deep"
30. Charlie's Angles Logo and Exploding

Charlie's Angels As Stock Footage!

Outtakes from "Angels in Paradise" (#23) were used in the series pilot movie "Waikiki." A close-up of Kelly's foot from "The Seance" (#11) was used as a close-up of Donna Mills foot.

And Tanya Roberts had a guest starring role in the film.

#97—ISLAND ANGELS
Third Hawaii Episode
December 7, 1980

CASE: Two Red Circle assassins are loose in Hawaii and using a singles club for their cover.

COVERS:
Kelly: Herself
Kris: Cocktail server
Julie: Photographer for "Single Life" Magazine
Bosley: Reporter for "Single Life" Magazine

FACTS:
Kelly's Hawaiian car is Red.

FASHIONS:
In almost every other scene the Angels are gracing the screen with very small fashionable clothing.

STAR SIGHTING
Barbi Benton as Toni Green
Richard Jaeckel as Bud Fisher
Carol Lynley as Lisa Gallo
Randolph Mantooth as Mark Williams
Soon-Teck Oh as Lt. Torres

Writer: Robert George
Story: Robert I. Holt
Director: Don Chaffey
Producer: Robert Janes

Bosely's Infamous Quote$!

"Time is money"
"Unfunny"
"Very profitable"
"No client, No fee"
"Not in the Budget"
"No, you can't keep it, Kelly"
"It's getting expensive"
"I'll take the check"

Angel Facts:
Chorus Line Angels (#104) is the only episode David Doyle directed.

#98—WAIKIKI ANGELS
Fourth Hawaii Episode
January 4, 1981

CASE: A congressman's daughter is kidnapped. Angels become lifeguards to rescue the girl.

COVERS:
Kelly: Lifeguard
Kris: Lifeguard
Julie: Lifeguard

FACTS:
Charlie is known as a legendary lifeguard. The Angels passed the Hawaii lifeguard test. Charlie gives the Angels a couple of days off for a good job.

FASHIONS:
"Baywatch" what? The Angels graced those lifeguard suits way before those girls ever did!!

TIDBIT:
This is the only episode that all three Angels are seen in bikinis at the same time.

STAR SIGHTING:
Dan Haggerty as Bo Thompson
Soon-Teck Oh as Lt. Torre

Writer: B.W. Sandefur
Director: Dennis Donnelly
Producer: Robert Janes

ALL NEW HAWAIIAN EPISODE!
TERROR STRIKES WAIKIKI BEACH! CAN THE ANGELS STRIKE BACK?
CHARLIE'S ANGELS
abc 7PM 17 19 38

#99—HULA ANGELS
Fifth & Final Hawaii Episode
January 11, 1981

CASE: A nightclub owner with a long list of enemies is kidnapped and is being held for a $1 million ransom.

COVERS:
Kelly: Detective
Kris: Go-go dancer
Julie: Go-go dancer
Bosley: Magazine writer

FACTS:
The Angels give Bosley a present, a native Hawaii grass skirt.

FASHIONS:
The Angel's strutting their final Hawaiian bathing suits for the office.

TIDBITS:
This was the final Hawaii episode.

STAR SIGHTING:
Joanna Cassidy as Stacie Parrish
Gene Barry as Steve Moss
Soon-Teck Oh as Lt. Torre

Written: Robert George
Director: Kim Manners
Producer: Robert Janes

Employee Angel Card: Julie Rogers

Born: New York, NY

Family: Parents: deceased

Schooling: Streets of NYC and spent time in prison for shoplifting then got her act together and graduated from a modeling school.

Address: Apartment, Marina Del Rey

Employment: Private Eye - partner Harry Stearns; Townsend Detective Agency, Los Angeles, CA 1980-1981

Awards: 1980- Given a special detective badge

Nickname: None

Pets: None

Boyfriends: None

Marriage: Single

Best Friends: Kelly Garrett, Kris Munroe, John Bosley, Harry Stearns (#94)

Car: Los Angeles: Ford Pinto - Orange/Red company car, Hawaii: Ford Jeep - yellow — company car

Interests: Scuba diving, dancing

Best Detective Skills: Streetwise and fetching in a bikini.

Haven't we seen you before?
The stock footage of the audience from "Angels on Ice" (#24) was re-used for both "Pretty Angels All in a Row" (#25) & "Mr. Galaxy" (#108)

#100—MOONSHININ' ANGELS
(aka: Shine On Angels & Shine On Angel Moon)
January 24, 1981

CASE: The 100-year long feud between two moonshine families starts up again after the NY mob wants to shut them down.

COVERS:
Kelly: Moonshine Driver
Kris: Still Master
Julie: Waitress
Bosley: High roller from Texas

FACTS:
The feuding families decide to make up and begin producing gasahol.
Kris and Kelly also get into the family feuding and argue over which family produces the best whiskey.

FASHIONS:
Thank the powers to be these Angels are all clothed! After getting back from Hawaii they were really cold!

Writer: B.W. Sandefur
Director: Kim Manners
Producer: Elaine Rich

#101—HE MARRIED AN ANGEL
January 31, 1981

CASE: A scam artist has defrauded two women out of their life savings.

COVERS:
Kelly: Monica's friend
Kris: Professional con woman
Julie: A reporter
Bosley: Kris's Texas con

FACTS:
Bosley is in search for a woman with a heart. Bill the bank manager is a friend of Charlie's.

FASHIONS:
Kris is spotted in her sexy black dress. The scam artist comes knocking for some sugar. How sweet.

Writer: Edward J. Lakso
Director: Don Chaffee
Producer: Edward J. Lakso

#102—TAXI ANGELS
February 7, 1981

CASE: The Archer Cab company is plagued by a string of accidents.

COVERS:
Kelly: Cab driver/ #7310
Kris: Waitress
Julie: Dispatcher

FACTS:
Kelly once again has bad luck with cars as she loses her brakes while driving a cab.

STAR SIGHTING:
Sally Kirkland as Laurie Archer
Norman Alden as Jake Barnett

TIDBITS:
As Kelly and Julie chase Jake Barnett, they have no guns. However, when they force him to stop, they pull guns out the air to apprehend him. Julie picks the lock to Sarge's apartment, yet in previous episodes Kelly is the pick expert.

Writer: Robert George
Director: John Peyser
Producer: Robert Janes

New Night For The Angels...In A Con Game To End All Con Games!

Have You Seen The 1981 Angels In Action?
CHARLIE'S ANGELS abc **7:00PM** ⑰ ⑲ ㊳
A-16 TV GUIDE

Angel Fact:
Tanya Roberts was a brunette when hired for the role of Julie Rogers but producers had her change her hair color to become the red headed Angel!

Lt. Mike Torres
When the Angels moved to Hawaii they worked closely with the Ohu Police Departments, Lt Mike Torres. Torres was played by actor Soo-Teck Oh who was featured on all five Hawaii episodes.

Original Episode Titles

Some of the best known episode titles were changed before they aired on television. Here is a list of some of the titles changes.

Titles	Original Titles
#5 - Target: Angels	Sudden Death
#11 - The Seance	Medium Cool
#12 - Angels on Wheels	Death on Wheels
#19 - Dancing in the Dark	Fast Dance on a Slow Mountain
#21 - Angels at Sea	The Short Voyage Home
#25 - Pretty Angels All in a Row	Along Came the Spider
#48 - Angel Come Home	Angels on Fire
#56 - Rosemary, For Remembrance	An Angel Called Rosemary
#74 - Caged Angel	Caged Animal
#93 - Angels in Hiding & To See an Angel Die	Street Models to Hawaiian Angels
#99 - Moonshinin' Angels	Shine on Angels

GUM CARD AD!

Remember Charlie's Angels Gum Cards???? Everyone had them, and today the cards are one of the most sought after collectibles.

This is the original order from which a store would fill out for their order.

The packets were only 10cents each and had six cards and one stick of bubble gum!

There were four sets of Charlie's Angels cards made by TOPPS in 1977.

Here's some trivia -- what was the very first gum card in the series??? A card featuring Kate Jackson and Farrah Fawcett and read "A Job Well Done"!

#103—ANGELS ON THE LINE
February 14, 1981

CASE: A woman has been murdered at the Hotline Club, and Kelly becomes the next target for the killer.

COVERS:
Kelly: The killer's bait
Kris: Club guest
Julie: Club guest

FASHIONS:
The Angels looking great in their club clothes. Yet it's the hypnotist that looses her hair...oh sorry, his hair.

TIDBITS:
Watch how a mud puddle appears out of nowhere for Margot/Paul to slip into.
This is the first time the Angels were tricked by a man in drag.

Writer: Edward J. Lakso
Director: Kim Manners
Producer: Edward J. Lakso

#104—CHORUS LINE ANGELS
February 21, 1981

CASE: A Vegas bound musical is plagued with problems starting with a missing choreographer and lead star.

COVERS:
Kelly: Dancer
Kris: Reporter for "Omaha Dance Review"
Julie: Kelly's Agent

FASHIONS:
Kelly brushes off her dancing shoes and her really tight leotard! Work it dancing Angel.

TIDBITS:
David Doyle hopped out of Bosely's office chair and into the directing chair for this episode. This marks the only episode that a cast member directed.
This was the second musical episode that was done. Although "Angels in the Wings" (#32) showcased musical songs, this episode showcased full dance numbers that demonstrated Jaclyn Smith's dancing ability.

Writer: Edward J. Lakso
Director: David Doyle
Producer: Edward J. Lakso

#105—STUNTWOMEN ANGELS
(aka: Angel on the Roof)
February 28, 1981

CASE: Movie sets are being terrorized by a mad archer who dresses up like Robin Hood.

COVERS:
Kelly: Stuntwoman
Kris: Stuntwoman
Julie: Stuntwoman

FACTS:
The Angels studied at "Big Teddy's Stunt School"

SIMILAR EPISODE:
#32 Angels in the Wings

FASHIONS:
The Angels looking so Hollywood flying around the set in those oh, "so tight" Robin Hood outfits! Good night sweet prince.
Gerald S. O'Loughlin also played in another Spelling/Goldberg show - **The Rookies**.

Writer: Edward J. Lakso
Director: Dennis Donnelly
Producer: Edward J. Lakso

#106 - ATTACK ANGELS
June 3, 1981

CASE: All the top executives at Western Techtronics are mysteriously dying off.

COVERS:
Kelly: Junior executive
Kris: Junior executive
Julie: Hypnotized secretary

FACTS:
Bosley finds candles to be very relaxing.

FASHIONS:
Julie is spotted in a bathing suit submerged in a water tank during her final stages of hypnosis...your getting very sleepy......very sleepy.

TIDBIT:
This is the only episode that the Angels are seen fighting each other. As Julie is hypnotized, Kelly and Kris try to stop her from killing their client. This action packed scene shows that these heavenly creatures are truly ready for the WWF.

STAR SIGHTING:
Eric Braeden as John Reardon
Dr. Joyce Brothers as Dr. Lantry

Writer: B.W. Sandefur
Director: Kim Manners
Producer: Elaine Rich

#107—ANGEL ON A ROLL
June 10, 1981

CASE: A computer designer of ATMS borrows money from various banks to support his gambling.

COVERS:
Kris: The bait
Kelly & Juile: Themselves

FACTS:
Kris's favorite painting is Van Gogh's "Wheat Field".
Kris falls for the robber Ted Markham.

FASHIONS:
Kris tries on all those diamonds that Ted wants to buy for her. Diamonds are a girls best friend!

Writer: Edward J. Lakso
Director: Kim Manners
Producer: Edward J. Lakso

#108—MR. GALAXY
June 17, 1981

CASE: Several murder attempts have been made on a body builder who is going for the "Mr. Galaxy" title.

COVERS:
Kelly: Reporter for "Heath Fair"
Kris: Bodyguard
Julie: Personal Trainer

FACTS:
Bosley receives a personal gym set from the client.

FASHIONS:
With all those bodybuilders muscles the Angels are in awe! Yet, the bodybuilders are the ones showcasing the tiny swimsuits on this case.

STAR SIGHTING:
Roger Callard as Ron Gates

Writer: Mickey Rich
Director: Don Chaffey
Producer: Elaine Rich

#109—LET OUR ANGEL LIVE
Charlie's Angels final show!
June 24, 1981

CASE: During a stake out Kelly is shot while apprehending a criminal. She is rushed to the hospital where the Angels gather and reminiscence about previous cases.

COVERS:
Themselves

FACTS:
Charlie was in the operation room with Kelly.
Charlie was with the doctors when they informed the Angels that Kelly was going to be fine.

SIMILAR EPISODES:
#7 - To Kill An Angel
#68 - Angels Remembered

FASHIONS;
The Angels didn't lose Kelly but the audience said goodbye to them for the last time. Good Case Angels!

TIDBITS:
Kris makes a reference to the episode "Terror on Ward One" from the first season. Maybe her sister Jill told her about the case!
Also while Kelly is recovering from surgery she is in full makeup!

Written: Edward J. Lakso
Director: Kim Manners
Producer: Kim Manners

Angel Fact:

Kate Jackson and Cheryl Ladd were the only Angels who worked on screen together prior to Charlie's Angels! The project was a Spelling-Goldberg production called **Satan School for Girls** in 1973! Jackson did return for the 2000 re-make which once again was produced by Aaron Spelling. This time around she played the dean of the school.

Jaclyn Smith worked with John Forsythe in the 1978 Spelling-Goldberg film titled, **The Users!**

Jaclyn Smith & Cheryl Ladd both made guest appearances on Kate Jackson's series **The Rookies**; however neither Angel had any scenes with Kate.

NIELSON RATINGS!

Charlie's Angels ruled the small screen from 1976 to 1979. It was season five when the series lost the rating wars and came in at #59. It's not really known why the series lost it's ratings hold. A lot could have been due to the series schedule. ABC moved the series from it's regular day on Wednesdays to Sundays. After the move to Sundays, ratings decreased. ABC then moved the Angels to Saturdays. After little ratings change, the series went on a hiatus — and returned the summer of 1981 on Wednesdays to play the final five episodes.

September 1976-April 1977

1	Happy Days	ABC	31.5
2	Laverne & Shirley	ABC	30.9
3	ABC Monday Night Movie	ABC	26.0
4	M*A*S*H	CBS	25.9
5	**Charlie's Angels**	**ABC**	**25.8**
6	The Big Event	NBC	24.4
7	The Six Million Dollar Man	ABC	24.2
8	ABC Sunday Night Movie	ABC	23.4
	Baretta	ABC	23.4
	One Day at a Time	CBS	23.4
11	Three's Company	ABC	23.4

photo credit: Dennis Kendell Yates

September 1977-April 1978

1	Laverne & Shirley	ABC	31.6
2	Happy Days	ABC	31.4
3	Three's Company	ABC	20.3
4	60 Minutes	CBC	24.4
	Charlie's Angels	**ABC**	**24.4**
	All in theFamily	CBS	24.4
7	Little House on the Praire	NBC	24.1
8	Alice	CBS	23.2
	M*A*S*H	CBS	23.2
10	One Day at a Time	CB3	23.0

Angels with Toys

Kate Jackson & Cheryl Ladd pictured with some very cool collectibles from the series. Jackson with the Milton Bradley Board Game and Cheryl is ready for wet weather with the Rainy Day Set.

September 1978-April 1979

1	Laverne & Shirley	ABC	30.5
2	Three's Company	ABC	30.3
3	Mork	ABC	28.6
	Happy Days	ABC	28.6
5	Angie	ABC	26.7
6	60 Minutes	CBS	25.5
7	M*A*S*H	CBS	25.4
8	The Ropers	ABC	25.2
9	All in the Family	CBS	24.9
	Taxi	ABC	24.9
11	Eight is Enough	ABC	24.8
12	**Charlie's Angels**	**ABC**	**24.4**
13	Alice	ABC	23.2
14	Little House on the Prairie	NBC	23.1
15	ABC Sunday Nigh Movie	ABC	22.6

September 1979-April 1980

1.	60 minutes	CBS	28.4
2.	Three's Company	ABC	26.3
3.	That's Incredible	ABC	25.8
4.	Alice	CBS	25.3
	M*A*S*H	CBS	25.3
	Dallas	CBS	25.3
7.	Flo	CBS	24.4
8.	The Jeffersons	CBS	24.3
9.	The Dukes of Hazzard	CBS	24.1
10.	One Day at a Time	CBS	23.0
11.	Archie Bunker's Place	CBS	22.9
12.	Eight Is Enough	ABC	22.8
13.	Taxi	ABC	22.4
14.	House Calls	CBS	22.1
15.	Real Peopel	NBC	21.8
	Little House on the Praire	NBC	21.8
17.	Happy Days	ABC	21.7
18.	Chips	NBC	21.5
19.	Trapper John, M. D.	CBS	21.2
20.	**Charlie's Angels**	**ABC**	**20.9**

Dancin' Angels (#86) Call Sheet.

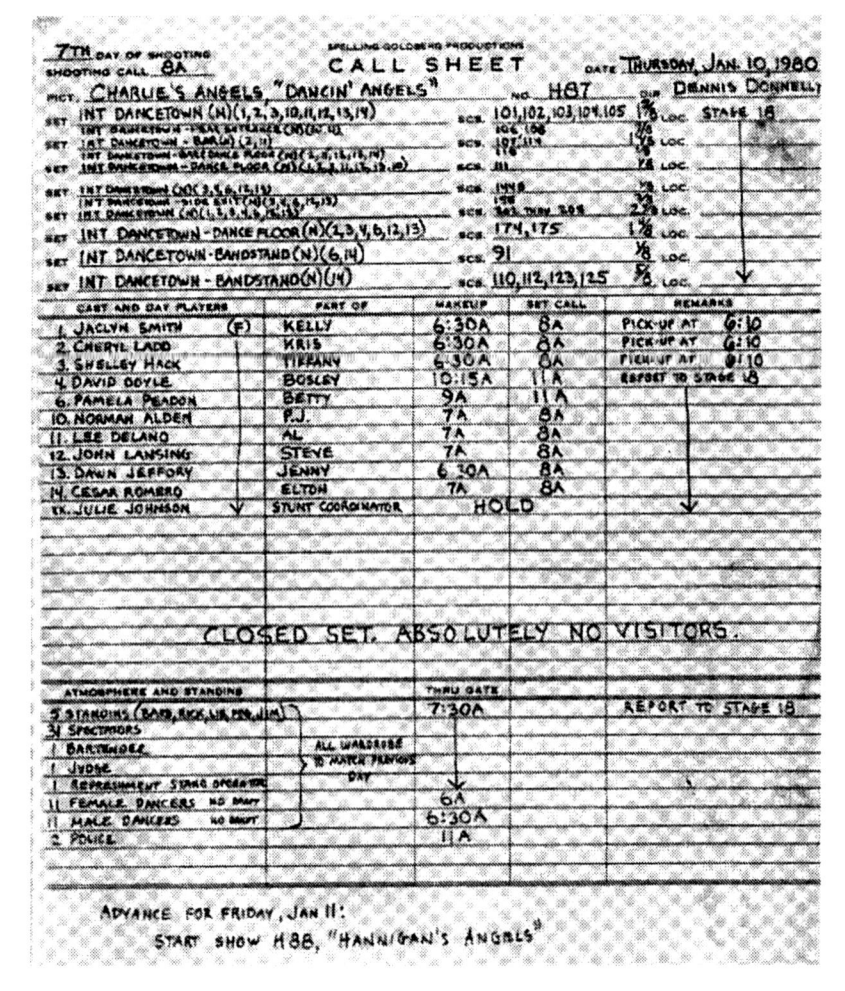

GUEST STARS!

Charlie's Angels, through out it's five year run, showcased famous and soon-to-be famous actors! Such stars as Dean Martin, Patrick Duffy, Barbara Stanwych, Tommy Lee Jones, Kim Basinger, Jamie Lee Curtis, just to name a few, graced the sound stage of **Charlie's Angels**!

Here are some highlights..

---

actress: KIM BASINGER

character: Linda Oliver

episode #4: "Angels in Chains" *season one*

description: Linda is a prisoner at the Pine Parish Prison farm. After being released she is hired as the receptionist for the Townsend Agency.

---

actor: DIRK BENEDICT

character:
Barton "Angels in Blue"
Denny Railsback "The Jade Trap"

episode:
#22 "The Blue Angels" *season one*
#44 "The Jade Trap" *second two*

description:
"The Blue Angels": Barton is a cop "on the take" who collects money from massage parlors for protection against police raids.

"The Jade Trap": Denny is a gigolo/sailing instructor who is after a jewel thief who saw him murder one of his clients.

---

actor: RENE AUBERJONOIS

Character:
Terrence "The Seance"
Freddie Fortune "Angels on Skates"

episode:
#11 "The Seance" *season one*
#77 "Angels on Skates" *season four*

description:
"The Seance" Terrance is a hypnotist who is spiriting away money from his customers.

"Angels on Skates" Freddie Fortune is the owner of Freddie's Roller World and has kidnapped a wealthy heiress.

---

actress: BARBI BENTON

character: Toni Green

episode #97: "Island Angels" *season five*

description: Toni Green is singles coordinator who helps the Angels track down a hired assassin.

---

actor SONY BONO

character: Marvin

episode #96: "Angels in the Deep" *season five*

description: Marvin is a hippie who is trying to turn a profit in selling "Maui Wowie"

actor   BARRY BOSTWICK

character: Ted Machlin

episode #44: "The Jade Trap" *season three*

description: Ted is a jewel thief who witnesses a murder while robbing a safe.

actor: ED BEGLEY JR.

character: Kenny Daniels

episode #77: "Angels on Skates" *season four*

description: Kenny is a professional roller skater involved with kidnapping his partner/girlfriend for her money.

actress: KIM CATTRALL

Character: Sharon Kellerman

episode #72: "Angels at the Altar" *season four*

Description: Sharon, a school friend of Kelly's is getting married. But she finds herself a client after her soon to be husband seems to be a target for a killer.

actress: JOANNA CASSIDY

character: Stacy

episode #99: "Hula Angels" *season five*

description: Stacy is a choreographer, and the ringmaster in the kidnapping of her boss for a $1,000,000 ransom.

actor: DENNIS COLE

character:
Tony Bordinay "Dancing in the Dark"
James Britten   "Unidentified Flying Angels"
Carl Hansworth "Terror on Skis"

episode:
#19 "Dancing in the Dark" *season one*
#29 "Unidentified Flying Angels" *season two*
#62 "Terror on Skis" *season three*

description:
"Dancing in the Dark" Tony is a disco instructor who on the side drugs up wealthy women and blackmails them with indecent photos.

"Unidentified Flying Angels" James Britten, a former astronaut is the center attraction of a rip off scheme based on contact with aliens.

"Terror on Skis" Carl Hansworth, a UN ambassador to the President, finds himself the target of a terrorist group and he falls in love with Kelly.

actor: GARY COLLINS

character:
Victor Buckley "Mother Angel"
Prof. Fairgate "Angels on Campus"

episode:
#55 Mother Angel, *season three*
#78 Angels On Campus, *season four*

description:
"Mother Angel" Victor Buckley is a murderer who is running away from his a bail bondsman and will kill anyone that stands in his way, even an Angel.

"Angel on Campus": Prof. Fairgate is kidnapping young girls from campus and selling them on the black market.

actor: TIMOTHY DALTON

charter: Damien Roth

episode #73 "Fallen Angel" *season four*

description: A "James Bond" type jewel thief. Damien is the boyfriend of Angel Jill Munroe. Jill turns a life of crime, in order to capture Damlen for Charlie.

actor: BERT CONVY

character: Paul Hollister

episodes #69: "Love Boat Angels" *season three*

description: Paul is a thief who steals from the rich and gives to the poor. As he is in the midst of retrieving stolen antiques he falls in love with Kris.

actress: JAMIE LEE CURTIS

character: Linda Frye

episode #51: "Winning is for Losers" *season three*

description: Linda is a professional golf player and is the best friend of Kris Munroe. Her life is put in jeopardy forcing Kris to wrestle with an alligator to save her.

actor: SAMMY DAVIS JR.

character: Sammy Davis Jr
Herbert Brubaker III

episode #34:
"Sammy Davis Jr. Kidnap Caper" *season two*

description:
Someone is trying to kidnap Sammy Davis Jr.; however the kidnappers grab Sammy's look-alike Herbert Brubaker III by mistake.

actor: PATRICK DUFFY

character: Bill Cord

episode #92-93: "One love....two Angels" *season four*

description: Bill Cord, is a lawyer for the millionaire client Olivier Barrows. He tracks down Barrow's long lost daughter, Kelly Garrett. Bill finds himself falling in love with Kelly and then with Kris. This leads to a huge fight between the two Angels; however after Bill is murdered the Angels feel they must find his killer.

actor: DAN HAGGERTY

character: Bo Thompson

episode #98: "Waikiki Angels" *season five*

description: Bo Thompson is the leader of a gang terrorizing beaches of Waikiki and begins to kidnap women.

actor: RICHARD JAECKEL

character: Bud Fischer

episode #97: "Island Angels" *season five*

description: Bud Fisher is a man with a mysterious past who has something to hide.

actor: DON HO

character: himself

episodes #23: "Angels In Paradise" *season two*

description: Don Ho is an old friend of Charlie's with whom Sabrian met with for help.

actor: BO HOPKINS

character:
Beau Creel "Charlie's Angels Pilot"
Wes Anderson "Love Boat Angels"

episode:
Charlie's Angels pilot movie
#69 "Love Boat Angels" *season three*

description:
pilot movie: Beau Creel is the driving force with the killing of Vincent LeMare.

"Love Boat Angels": Wes Anderson is the partner of Paul Hollister, a professional thief.

actor: CASEY KASEM

character: Tom Rogers

episode #51: "Winning is for Losers" *season three*

description: Tom Rogers is a sports reporter covering the golf match.

actress: SALLY KIRKLAND

character:
Lonnie "Caged Angel"
Laurie Archer "Taxi Angels"

episodes : #74
"Caged Angel" *season four*
episode: #102
"Taxi Angels" *season five*

descriptions:
"Caged Angel" Lonnie is a prisoner who helps Kris try to escape from the grips of Big Aggie.

"Taxi Angels" Laurie Archer owns Archer Cab Company and hires the Angels to investigate accidents with her cab company.

---

actress: AUDREY LANDERS

character: Donna

episode #64: "Teen Angels" *season three*

description: Donna is a spoiled rich girl who blackmails her friends into selling drugs and alcohol.

---

actress: JOANNA KERNS

character: Natalie

episode #22: " The Blue Angels" *season one*

description: She is a young prostitute beaten in Paradise massage parlor and the only witness to a murder.

---

actor: TOMMY LEE JONES

character: Aram Kolegian

episode: CHARLIE'S ANGELS pilot

description: Aram is a farm hand who discovers the Angels secret and comes to rescue when the Angels are being hunted down one by one.

---

actress: JUDY LANDERS

characters:
Mrs. Chicken " Angels on the Run"
Linen girl "Love Boat Angels"

episodes
#45: "Angels on the Run" *season two*
#69: "Love Boat Angels" *season four*

descriptions:
"Angels on the Run": Mrs. Chicken delivers Bosely's lunch, but it's the wrong order. Bosely wants breasts and Mrs. Chicken brings him legs!

" Love Boat Angels": A new linen girl shows up at the agency. However Kris and Kelly mistake her for new Angel, Tiffany Welles.

actress: IDA LUPINO

character: Gloria Gibson

episode #20: "I Will Be Remembered" *season one*

description: Gloria Gibson, a former star, is recreating a film comeback. Someone is staging scenes from her movies making her believe she is going insane.

actress: ROBIN MATTSON

character: Erica Burke

episode #81: "Of Ghosts and Angels" *season four*

description: Erica, an old college friend of Tiffany's who recently married. Erica begins to feel there is something wrong with the house. Something or someone does not want her there.

actor: CRAIG T. NELSON

character: Stone

episode #45: "Angels on the Run" *season two*

description: Stone is one of the gangsters trying to track down their lost diamonds.

actor: DEAN MARTIN

character: Frank Howell

episode #47: "Angels in Vegas" *season three*

description: Frank Howell is a casino owner who hires the Angels to find who wants to put him out of business. Sabrina and Frank fall head over heals in love.

actress: SARAH PURCELL

character: Millicent Krail

episode #65: "Marathon Angels" *season three*

description: Millicent Krail is a reporter covering the marathon for a news station.

actor: ROBERT REED

character: Glenn Staley

episode #92-93: "One Love...Two Angels" *season four*

description: Glenn Staley is the man behind the death of his Uncle Oliver while trying to take control of his estate.

actor: CESAR ROMERO

character: Elton Mills

episode #86: "Dancin' Angels" *season four*

description: Elton Mills is a conductor of the big band at a dancing marathon. The gentle conductor is killing dancers so the audience can appreciate his music.

actor: PHIL SILVERS

character: Max

episode #24: "Angels on Ice" *season two*

description: Max is the owner of an ice skating show who hires the Angels after the stars of the ice show end up missing.

actor: TOM SELLECK

character: Dr. Alan Samuelson

episode #5 "Target Angels" *season one*

description: Dr. Alan Samuelson is the boyfriend of Kelly Garrett. When an assassin attempts to kill Kelly, she makes the good doctor get out of harms way.

actor: DICK SARGENT

character:
Hugh Morris "Angels on Wheels"
Marty Cole "Angels in Vegas"
James Avery "Love Boat Angels"

episode:
#12 "Angels on Wheels" *season one*
#47 "Angels in Vegas" *season three*
#69 "Love Boat Angels" *season four*

descriptions:
"Angels on Wheels" Hugh Morris the owner of the roller skating derby team.

"Angels in Vegas" Marty Cole, a Vegas night club singer, turns out to be a ruthless killer.

"Love Boat Angels" James Avery is a client that wants to get the museum antiques back from the thieves.

actress: BARBARA STANWYCK

character: Antonia "Toni" Blake

episode #91: "Toni's Boys" *season four*

description: Antonia runs "Toni's Boys", a male version of *Charlie's Angels*. Her boys are hired to protect the Angels from a hit man.

actress: JANE WYMAN

character: Eleanor Willard

episode #95: "To See an Angel Die" *season five*

description: Eleanor Willard finds Kris' car abandoned. Eleanor is a psychic and helps the Angels find Kris before she is killed.

actress: LAUREN TEWES

characters:
Christine Hunter "Angels in Chains"
Julie McCoy "Love Boat Angels"

episode:
#4 "Angels in Chains" *season one*
#69 "Love Boat Angels" *season four*

description:
"Angels in Chains" Christine has not heard from her sister for a couple of weeks and feels that there has been foul play. She hires the Angels to find her sister in Pine Parish Prison.

"Love Boat Angels" Julie McCoy is the cruise director on "The Love Boat" and welcomes the Angels aboard.

actor ROBERT URICH

character: Dan Tana

episode #47: "Angels in Vegas" *season three*

description: Dan Tana, a Vegas private eye, bumps into Bosely and the Angels as they are on their way back to Los Angeles.

Angel Toys

Charlie's Angels merchandise was heavily marketed during the 1977 and 1978 TV seasons. After 3 million lunch boxes and 4 million dolls were sold, **Charlie's Angels** shot a name for themselves in the toy world. Little girls and boys could emulate the Angels style with Dress-Up Kits, Sunglasses and Hair Care Sets. They could also learn to shoot like an Angel with Target Sets, and even communicate with each other via Walkie-Talkies. Crime didn't stand a chance!

Today, all these various toys are very collectable. Items that once cost $1.50 can now go for hundreds of dollars. Here is just sample of some of the many products that were released on the Angelic trio.

Danger by Day....GLAMOUR by night.....

CHARLIE'S ANGELS
HIDEAWAY HOUSE

4800 The Charlie's Angels Hideaway House (Ages 4-12)
Super-chic, ultra-contemporary... it's the "heavenly abode" Charlie had built for his Angels! And what's more the Hideaway House revolves 360° to follow the path of the sun! There are three levels that make up the Hideaway House: a roof-top sun deck complete with umbrella; the mid-level houses the kitchen and living room area that includes a table, couch, director's chair and bar stool; the lower level has been designed for cookouts and there's an exercise area for keeping fit. (Assembly Required)
5¾" x 22¾" x 21½" PACK: 4 pcs.
WT.: 30 lbs. CU.FT.: 6.1

4801 Charlie's Angels Deluxe Hideaway House
Same as above, also includes Jill, Sabrina and Kelly with jumpsuits and boots, plus "Black Magic", "Peasantry" and "Midnight Flight" wardrobe outfits.
5¾" x 22¾" x 21½" PACK: 4 pcs. WT.: 32 lbs. CU.FT.: 6.1

Hasbro Toy Catalogues 1977 & 1978

These are the original pages from the Hasbro 1977 & 1978 catalogues which showcased the Charlie's Angels doll line!

The new Angel Kris was introduced in the 1978 line.

CHARLIE'S ANGELS
BEAUTIFUL GIRLS WHO LIVE DANGEROUSLY!

All the excitement and glamour of TV's most popular action show comes alive in Hasbro's Charlie's Angels dolls and accessories!

Angelic Heaven

1978 finds Hasbro looking forward to another "Year of the Angel"

Introducing Kris... Charlie's newest Angel

NEW

4850 Charlie's Angels — Kris (Ages 4-12)
4860 Charlie's Angels — Jill
4861 Charlie's Angels — Sabrina
4862 Charlie's Angels — Kelly
Charlie's Angels get beautiful support from Kris this year, the newest angel who made her TV debut this Fall. All Angels stand 8½" tall. Fully jointed and poseable with "twist 'n turn" waist. Long, combable hair. Jumpsuit, boots.
1½ x 8½ x 11⅞" PACK: 12 pcs. WT.: 7 lbs. CU. FT.: .5

4863 Charlie's Angels Doll Assortment
Includes 12 of Kris, 6 of Sabrina and 6 of Jill.
1½ x 8½ x 11⅞" PACK: 24 pcs. WT.: 9 lbs. CU. FT.: 1.2

Golden Marathon Girl — Golden Pro — Golden Sport
Golden Intrigue — Golden Whispers — Golden Goddess

4840 Charlie's Angels Gold Coast Edition **NEW**

• **Golden Whispers:** Soft and romantic white eyelet dress with fringed shawl. Golden slippers, rose choker.
• **Golden Intrigue:** Blazing raincoat for undercover work. A scarf for dash, plus boots.
• **Golden Goddess:** a 24 carat look. Swimsuit, slacks, slippers.
• **Golden Marathon Girl:** Silky, plum jogging togs with golden stripes, plus sneakers.
• **Golden Sport:** Athletic outfit sparkled up with a midas touch. Sneakers, too.
• **Golden Pro:** The gilded tennis look. Tennis dress with visor with golden trim. Includes sneakers.

11 x 9 x ¾" PACK: 24 pcs. WT.: 12 lbs. CU. FT.: 1.1

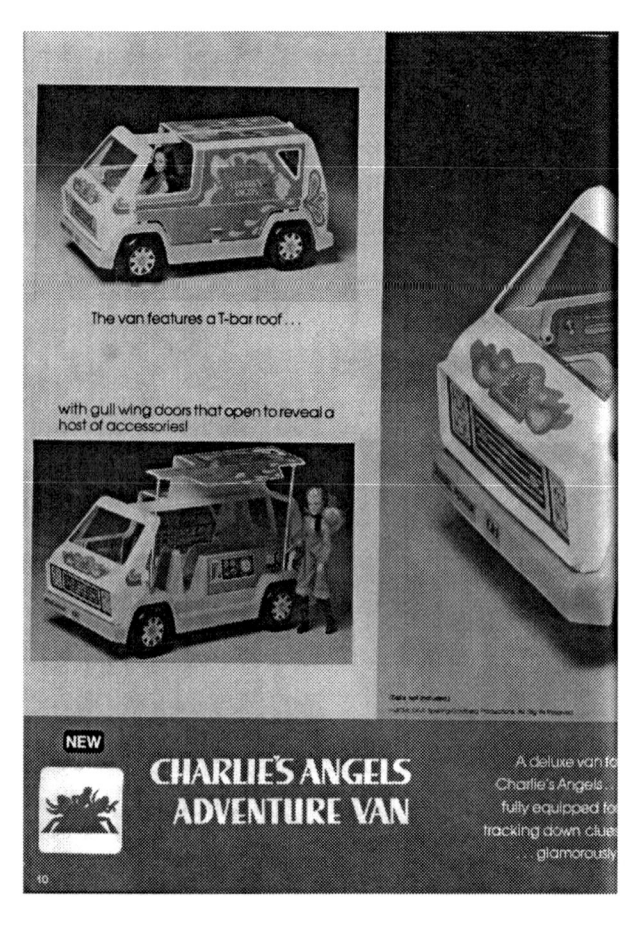

The van features a T-bar roof...

with gull wing doors that open to reveal a host of accessories!

NEW

CHARLIE'S ANGELS ADVENTURE VAN

A deluxe van for Charlie's Angels... fully equipped for tracking down clues... glamorously

4890 Charlie's Angels Van (Ages 4 to 12)
A super deluxe custom van for Charlie's Angels' glamourous adventures! Splashed with vibrant colors... nothing but the most luxurious for Charlie's girls. Features T-bar roof, gull wing doors that reveal a secret control panel with headset, bucket seats, parson's table and director's chair inside. Also includes binoculars and a camera for surveillance work. Couch inside opens to provide storage space. (Assembly Required.)
5½ x 8½ x 16" PACK: 4 pcs. WT.: 8 lbs. CU. FT.: 2.7

154

4878 Fashion Tote (Ages 4-12)
A very unique, cylindrical fashion tote for danger's darlings! Housed in the lid is an area for hanging the girl's clothes (3 hangers included) plus room for an Angel or two!
8 x 9"   PACK: 6 pcs.   WT: 8 lbs.   CU. FT.: 1.1
(Doll not included)

4876 Charlie's Angels Flying Skateboard
(Ages 4 to 12)
The girls live dangerously as they become skateboard super sleuths! Jill makes a hair-raising escape atop a real, miniature skateboard, looking as delightful as ever in cut-offs, sweatshirt and sneakers.
5 x 5 x 10½"   PACK: 12 pcs.   WT: 3 lbs.   CU. FT.: .6
(Doll not included)

Los Angeles De Charlie
(by LiliLedy)

Angel dolls released in Mexico with a different style box.

Fashion Tote
(by Hasbro)

This case was perfect for any Angel on assignment! The Fashion Tote holds your "Angel" doll and all it's accessories.

Doll Refund Check
This is a 50 cent refund check. If you bought a Charlie's Angels doll you could get some change back! Just fill it out and send it in before September 30, 1977.

Hasbro
50¢ refund
ON YOUR FIRST PURCHASE OF ANY
CHARLIE'S ANGELS doll

Angelic Heaven

Charlie's Angels Dolls
(by Hasbro)

Here are the 4 heavenly dolls which keep the toy box free of crime! Sabrina, Kelly, Jill and Kris. Each doll came in a colorful jump suit that matched their car color.

Sabrina in Red
Kelly in Yellow
Jill in White.

Except Kris who came dressed in a heavenly green jumpsuit!

Charlie's Angels Gift Set (by Hasbro)
The set came with all three dolls in a special pack. There were two gift sets released, one with Sabrina, Kelly & Jill, and then with Kris, Kelly & Sabrina.

Droles De Dames Dolls
(by Rayland)

Released in France, the Angels had a new box design but still had the same high-fashion jumpsuits!

156

Hide-A-Way House
(by Hasbro)
The Hide-A-Way House is where the Angels find a little R&R. When together it stands over 30 inches tall and comes complete with 3 levels. A perfect place for any Angel to hang out! It came in both a Kris and Jill version.

Mail-Order Dolls
(by Hasbro)
The packaging for the mail order dolls were different than what appeared on the store shelves. You would receive a doll in one of these boxes when ordering from Wards, JcPenny's or Sears.

Adventure Van
(by Hasbro)

It was a van FULL of heavenly adventure for the Charlie's Angels dolls! It also included head sets, table, chairs and a secret panel!

BECOME A CHARTER MEMBER
OF THE OFFICIAL
Charlie's Angels™
FAN CLUB
LOOK AT EVERYTHING YOU GET WHEN YOU JOIN!
THESE ITEMS CAN NOT BE BOUGHT IN A STORE
1. 8" Charlie's Angels
Color Iron-On Decal
(T-Shirt Not Included)
Charlie's Angels
OFFICIAL
FAN CLUB MEMBERSHIP CARD
3. Official Wallet Size
Membership Card
THIS IS TO CERTIFY THAT
NAME
IS A MEMBER IN GOOD STANDING OF THE OFFICIAL CHARLIE'S ANGELS FAN CLUB AND IS ENTITLED TO ALL OF THE BENEFITS THEREOF
AUTHORIZATION
4. 8"x10" Official
Membership Scroll
JOIN NOW!
Get an actual 35mm Film Clip right from the actual show, Only Members of this Club will have them. These clips are in full color and can be reproduced for wallet or any size print.
2. 8"x10" Autographed
Glossy Photograph
©MCMLXXVII Spelling-Goldberg Productions
5. 16"x20" 4-Color
Poster (cannot be bought in a store.)
Please enroll me as a charter member of the Official CHARLIE'S ANGELS FAN CLUB and send me all of the above merchandise.
Enclose cash, check or money order for each Fan Club membership fee.
☐ 1 year membership $5.00
NAME
ADDRESS
CITY
STATE
ZIP
TE1
Be the first in your neighborhood to be a Charlie's Angels Fan Club Member. Receive notices of upcoming events, special offers for members only, plus so many other exciting special offers...plus a chance to win an all expenses paid trip to California and tour of the studio.
SEND $5.00 to:
CHARLIE'S ANGELS FAN CLUB
P.O. BOX #370 NANUET, N.Y. 10954
© MCMLXXVII Spelling-Goldberg Productions, All Rights Reserved
HAVE YOUR FRIENDS JOIN
Just have them print their name & address on a 3"x4" card and send it to us along with their $5.00 membership fee.

Charlie's Angels Fashion Dress-Up Set
(HG Toys)
This box set included a set of high heels, belt, sunglasses, purse and a watch. A must for any Angel night on the town.

Cosmetic Beauty Kit
(by Hasbro)
This beautiful box set holds everything to make an Angel sparkle out on a case. Contains: mirror, nail polish, makeup, manicure set, a cosmetic purse and Charlie's Angels Beauty Tips.

Beauty Hair Care Set
(by HG Toys)

Angels you must be ready at a moments notice!! So the Beauty Hair Care Set is sure to come in very handy!

It has a hair blower (which works); mirror, roller bag & rollers brush. PLUS makeup tips for each Angel and a mini-poster so you can look just like your favorite Angel!

Adventure By Day
Glamour By Night Box Sets
(by Hasbro)

These doll outfits each held an adventure and a glamour out fit for the night.

Sabrina: Slalom Caper - Ski adventure
Kelly: Underwater Intrigue - deep sea diving adventure
Jill: River Race - river rafting adventure

Paint By Numbers Sets (by Hasbro)

The regular edition came with two "paint by numbers" pictures and 6 heavenly acrylic paints.

The "deluxe" edition came with 3 pictures and 9 acrylic paints to create the heavenly adventures.

Colorforms:
Adventure Set
(by Colorforms)
Inside held the heavenly plastic stickers which could be placed on a high adventure backdrop.

160

**The Charlie's
Angels Storybook.**
(By Golden All Star Books) 1977

Four **English Annuals** for the first 4 years of the series - England (by Stafford Pemberton)

**"It Takes A Thief"
Children Book**
This children's book produced in England showcases a story starring Kris, Kelly & Sabrina.

Patch (maker unknown)

Got a rip??? Well, let Charlie's Angels cover it! This great patch was made in England and showcased Jill, Sabrina and Kelly! They Got You Covered!

CHARLIE'S ANGELS

Beautiful girls who live dangerously.

TV advertising

Charlie's Angels is the hottest show to hit the TV screen in years, and we've got the Angels 8½" high and advertised to the whole nation. And each display has the special 50¢ refund offer, too. When the smoke clears, Charlie's "little" Angels, Jill, Kelly, and Sabrina, will be the darlings of America, and folks will burn up the pavement getting to your store.

Billboard

you don't whisper about it; you shout it the crossroads of the world.

in action for '77.
CHARLIE'S ANGELS
Beautiful girls who live dangerously.

Glamourous, Blazing Motion Display

Brighten up your sales appeal with this 3-dimensional flashing burst that rotates to catch your customer's eye featuring Charlie's Angels and their fashion line.

© 1977, Spelling-Goldberg Productions. All rights reserved.

Fleetwood Toys
Fleetwood made over 30 different styles of Charlie's Angels items on cards. Such as Travelers; Shoulder Bag & the hair dryer with versions featuring Jill & Kris.

Charlie's Angels Mirrors
Three different styles which showcased Jill, Sabrina & Kelly.

Now! Get these Heavenly Values from Charlie's Angels

Ride with Charlie's Angels!
Imagine—an authentic scale model Mobile Unit Van that's an exact copy of one of the vehicles Charlie's Angels travel in! This detailed Revell Model Kit includes custom interior with bed, icebox, TV, stereo speakers, bubble sun roof and vent, 2-position rear doors, tinted portholes, bucket seats, CB antenna and much, much more! You'll have hours of fun building this exciting model, playing with it and showing it off to your friends!
Code 961 **Only $6.00, postpaid**

Be One of Charlie's Angels
Here's an exciting, authentic Charlie's Angels costume, complete with full face mask of Sabrina! Costume features colorful flame-retardant tunic with elasticized waistband and bright red and black design. Fits children 8 to 10 years old (47" to 52" tall).
Code 979 **Only $4.50, postpaid**

Shoot Targets with Charlie's Angels!
Two realistic target guns and six safety darts let you have hours of fun shooting at a beautiful knockdown target—all in the official Charlie's Angels Target Set!
Code 897 **Only $5.50, postpaid**

Hang Charlie's Angels on Your Wall!
Giant 25" by 35" full-color poster features all three of Charlie's Angels—Sabrina, Chris and Kelly!
Code 381 **Only $2.50 postpaid**

Copy or clip out this coupon, complete it (be sure to get code numbers right), then mail your order today to:
Charlie's Angels Heavenly Offer
Dept. CA-2
6 Commercial Street, Hicksville, N.Y. 11801

YES! Rush me the Heavenly Charlie's Angels items checked here for 15 days' no-risk examination. If I'm not satisfied, I may return any of the items within 15 days for a complete refund. With that understanding, here's my check or money order for $ _____ (N.Y. and Conn. residents please include tax.)

☐ Charlie's Angels Mobile Unit Van, Code 961, **Only $6.00**
☐ Charlie's Angels Costume with Mask, Code 979, **Only $4.50**
☐ Charlie's Angels Giant Poster, Code 381, **Only $2.50**
☐ Charlie's Angels Target Set, Code 897, **Only $5.50**

Name _____
Address _____
City _____ State _____ Zip _____

Japanese Novels

The Charlie's Angels books where translated into Japanese. They even came with mini pull-out posters.

Charlie's Angels Books
(by BB)

Charlie's Angels was released with 5 books was five cases, the pilot, The Killing Kind, Angels on a String, Angels in Chains and Angels on Ice. All the books were written by Max Franklin.

"Drei Engel Fur Charlie" paper novels (by Goldmann)

These three rare heavenly books were produced in 1979 in Germany. The set is translated from the US version.

Novels from France & Greece

Two Novels from Brazil

Charlie's Angels Coloring Book
(by Stafford Pemberton)
This coloring book was produced in England. And showcased Kris, Kelly & Sabrina.

Press Out Book
(by Stafford Pemberton)

Another cloud 9 product from England! This rare collectable showcased Sabrina, Kelly & Kris in a fun press out adventure.

Poster Art Kit
(by HG Toys)
The poster art kit let any "Angel" be creative with using colorful markers to paint in 2 "angel" adventures. This was produced in both Jill & Kris versions and also came in a deluxe box set version.

Notebooks
(Stuart Hall Company, inc)
Did you need some heavenly guidance in school? The best bet was to take some Charlie's Angels notebooks with you. There were 3 versions.

Charlie's Angels Puzzles
(by HG Toys)

There where eight Charlie's Angels puzzles in the US. three 150 pieces for each cast and a Giant Puzzle with 250 pieces featuring Jill, Kelly & Sabrina and a 500 piece puzzle featuring Kris, Kelly & Sabrina.

Charlie's Angels English Puzzles
(by Stafford Pemberton)
There where two versions one set with Jill & the other set with Kris.

Drei Engel Fur Charlie
(by Revell)
This is the German release of the Charlie's Angels Model Kit. Which showcased Kris, Kelly & Sabrina. (US version featured Jill instead)

AM Wrist Radio
(by Illco)

Angels must stay in touch at all times!!! This might be the right thing to wear but it just might not match your outfit!

Charlie's's Angels Cups
(by Thermo-Serv)
Need a drink to go while staking out a bad guy? The perfect beverage holder would be a Charlie's Angles cup, mug or stein! The set of three showcased Kelly, Kris & Sabrina.

Charlie's Angels Lunch Box & Brunch Bag
(by Aladdin)
Remember taking the Angels to lunch??? Well, millions of kids did with these cool lunchbox and brunch bag. Both came with a cool thermos.

Topps Gum Cards
(by Topps)
Topps brought out 4 series of Charlie's Angels Cards which totaled 256 cards in a complete set. The cards showcased Sabrina, Kelly, Jill & Kris.

Charlie's Angels Monty Gum Cards
Monty Gum cards were produced in Holland. They are ultra rare and span the first 4 season of Angels (which includes Tiffany cards). These cards are about half the size of Topps cards produced in the U.S.

Charlie's Angels Topps Boxs
(by Topps)

Even the boxs for the gum cards were heavenly items. Each new series a new box was created.

Los Angeles deCharlie
(by Topps)

This was the only card set released in Mexico.

Feetwood Toys

This sales sheet showcases many of the Feetwood Toys which where made. All the Feetwood Toys came on cardboard backing with great images on the front. The company produced "Jewelry Sets" "Blow Dryer," "Talk Time," "Pendants," "Travelers" and the list goes on. Feetwood packaging featured images of Jill & Kris.

420-600

421-606

425-604

425-602

420-601

421-604

FLEETWOOD TOY CORPORATION INC. - 1115 BROADWAY, NEW YORK, N.Y. 10010 - TEL.: (212) 924-8888

STYLE NO. 8170
"CHARLIE'S ANGELS" DELUXE 3-PC. LUGGAGE SET
Now your favorite TV stars own luggage set—Kelly, Jill & Sabrina appear on models case in color. All vinyl construction. Beautifully gift boxed. Pack: 6 sets Wt: 23 lbs.
Contains: Train Case (9¼"x 6¼"x 5")
Models Case (10"x 10"x 5")
Day Tripper (16"x 10¾"x 3¼")

STYLE NO. 8240
"CHARLIE'S ANGELS" 3-PC. LUGGAGE SET
Television's most beautiful girls now have their very own luggage. All vinyl construction. New retail color box. Pack: 12 sets Wt: 25 lbs.
Contains: Train Case (8"x 4¼"x 3¾")
Models Case (7½"x 7½"x 3¼")
Day Tripper (12½"x 9¾"x 3¼")

Charlie's Angels Luggage (Travel Toy, Inc)

Here are the two versions of the Charlie's Angels Luggage. The Deluxe 3-pic Luggage Set and the regular 3-pc. luggage set.

3 Piece Luggage Set
(Travel Toy, Inc)

Have an undercover out of town?? Take your Charlie's Angels luggage with you! Each piece showcases the name of each Angel on it!

Charlie's Angels Paper Dolls
(by The Toy Factory)
These are the US version of the "Paper Dolls." Each Angel came in their own box, Sabrina, Kelly & Jill. The box contained one 14 inch cut-out Angel and "magic touch" rub on/peel off clothing.

Rainy Day Set
(by Travel Toy, Corp.)
An Angel never leaves the house without her "Rainy Day Set" which includes a rain hat, a water proof purse with a photo of the Angels and an umbrella complete with the "Angel" logo on it!

Pocketbook Radio: Communications Center
(by Illco toy)
This cool item was a transistorized radio with "mic" and earplug. It can pick up AM radio, perform morse code, and includes an earphone. A must to have to keep in touch with Sabrina, Jill or Kelly.

Doll Dressing Books
(by Stafford Pemberton)

3 versions of the English Doll Dressing Books were made in Kris, Sabrina and Kelly styles! Some of the books where made with just a paper doll and others contained both a doll and a storybook.

Charlie's Angels Pinball Machine
(by D. Gottlieb & Co)

This flyer to advertise the new 1978 Charlie's Angels pinball machine.

It was rumored that Spelling/Goldberg licensed the pinball machine just so they could have one for themselves.

Charlie's Angels Doll Fashions

(by Hasbro)
Six original fashions where released with the dolls. Two for each Angel.

Jill: Russian Roulette & Black Magic.
(Also reissued with Kris)
Kelly: Night Caper & Moonlight Flight.
Sabrina: Peasantry & Gaucho Pizazz

Gold Coast Edition

(by Hasbro)
Second set of six fashions were produced when the Kris Munroe doll was released.

Kris: Golden Goddess & Golden Whispers
Kelly: Golden Marathon Girl & Golden Pro
Sabrina. Golden Sport & Golden Intrigue

Droles De Dames Doll Outfits

(by Raynal)

Here is one of the doll clothing line from France. The packaging is done a bit different than the states.

Target Set
(by Palco toys)

The target set came in both Jill & Kris versions.

It allowed any Angel in training to do target practice with shooting a gun.

Charlie's Angels Board Game
(by Milton Bradley)
Want all the adventure at home? Well, the Charlie's Angels game is a perfect fit! All the adventure without leaving ones living room. The game was produced twice, once with Jill, Kelly & Sabrina and again when Kris joined the office.

Charlie's Angels Board Game
(by Milton Brady)

This game is in French & English and came in both Jill & Kris versions.

Charlie's Angels Play Set
(by The Toy Factory)
This is hours of fun...with cut outs of your favorite Angels & three different play sets. The set also includes cut outs of the Angels cars!

Toy Fashion Watch
(by GLJ Toys)
Every Angel needs to be on time and fashionable! This watch does it all and comes in both blue and pink. Plus the second hand is the "Charlie's Angels" logo which ticks back and forth!

Charlie's Angels Magic Slate
(by Whitman)

The Magic Slate is one of the rarest Angel collectibles. On the slate an "Angel" could write secret message to fellow "Angels" and erase it before the bad guys could read it!

Charlie's Angels Wallet
(by Travel Toy Corp.)
A must for all that money an Angel makes while working for Charlie. The wallet came with a photo of the Angels on the cover...how heavenly!

Angel Pin-On Buttons (by Hotline)
Show your "Angel" pride with a cool button! The buttons also came with separate images of Kris, Kelly & Sabrina

Hasbro Trade ad which introduced the Kris Munroe doll to store owners.

Angelic Heaven

Cover Girl Angels

Throughout the series of **Charlie's Angels,** the actresses together and separately appeared on virtually every magazine in the USA. After the series was syndicated throughout the world, the actresses found themselves on thousands more publications! Here are a small sampling of magazine covers which the actresses graced. These Angels were truly the "Supermodels" of the '70s!

Charlie's Angels Official
Poster Monthly
1977 - USA
Devoted to Charlie's Angels
folds out into a poster

Charlie's Angels Official
Poster Monthly
1977 - USA
Devoted to Charlie's Angels
folds out into a poster

Charlie's Angels Official
Poster Monthly
1977 - USA
Devoted to Charlie's Angels
folds out into a poster

**Charlie's Angels in Hawaii
USA - 1977
Devoted to Charlie's Angels**

**Super Pop: Los Angeles
De Charlie Poster
Devoted to Charlie's Angels
Spain - 1977**

**A Tribute to Charlie's
Angels
England - 1977
folds out into a poster
Devoted to Charlie's Angels**

178

People - December 6, 1976

People - August 15, 1977

People - September 26, 1977

People - September 18, 1978

People - October 9, 1978

People - June 4, 1979

People - September 24, 1979

People - February 2, 1981

People - October 20, 1986

Farrah and her Friends
1977 - USA

TV Super Shows 4
May 1977 - USA

TV Favorites
1977 - USA

Charlie's Angels Poster
Japan - 1980

Meet
England - 1977

Charlie's Angels TVStars
Australia

Toaphu
Greece

Toaphu
Greece

Toaphu
Greece

TV Plus
France

Il Monello
March 1981 - Italy

Il Monello
Italy - 1983

Look-in
England - July 1977

Look-in
England - 1978

Look-in
England - May 1980

TELEjunior
France

PreVIEW
April 1977 - USA

PreVIEW
May 1978 - USA

Angelic Heaven

TVGuide - USA - February 18-24, 1977	TVGuide - USA August 26 - Sept 1, 1978	TVGuide - USA Dec 29 1979 - Jan 4 1980
TVGuide - Australia July 7-13, 1979	TVGuide - Argentina - 1977	TVGuide - Australia May 10-16, 1980
TVGuide - Canada - 1980 Jan 31 - Feb 1, 1981	TVGuide - Canada - 1979 March 8-14, 1980	TVGuide - Japan

The Life and Times of Fabulous Farrah
March/April 1977
Devoted to Farrah

Girl of the Year Farrah
1977 - USA
Devoted to Farrah

Farrah Her Book
1977-USA
Devoted to Farrah

Maviva - Jaclyn Smith
1978 Greece

The Angels 1977 - USA
Devoted to Charlie's Angels

Japan - 1977

Katepiva
1980 - Greece

Oounep
1981 - Greece

Cheryl Ladd
November 1978 USA
Devoted to Cheryl

TV Star Parade
May 1978 - USA

TV Star Parade
November 1978 - USA

TV Star Parade
November 1979 - USA

TV Star Parade
November 1977 - USA

Movie Stars
June 1978 - USA

Movie Stars
November 1978 - USA

Rona Barrett's Gossip
September 1979 - USA

TV & Movie People
June 1979 - USA

May 1979 - Greece
Full Color Poster

Intimidades

Rona Barretts' Gossip
June 1978 - USA

Rona Barretts' Gossip
February 1978 - USA

Rona Barrett's Hollywood
March 1977 - USA

Wild World of Skateboarding
May 1977 - USA

PreView
August 1978 - USA

TV Superstar
Devoted to Charlie's Angels
June 1977 - USA

Bananas
1977 - USA

TV
Japan

Angel Locations

Welcome to Townsend Investigations! Though the office has long since closed it's doors, it looks almost the same as it did back in the 1970s. The only major changes are the expanded windows on the bottom floor. Today, it holds an appliance store.

The agency is located at 189 Robertson, Los Angeles

Here is the original Townsend office that was used in the series pilot. Still looking identical to how it did back then. Maybe Charlie forgot to tell Woodville the office moved?

The original agency is located at 8619 Sunset Blvd, West Hollywood

This is the Kelly Garrett house used in seasons 2-5. The house has stayed remarkably unchanged – all the way down to the style and color. If you look real closely, you may even see Kelly walk out the front door.

The house is a private residence located in Century City, Los Angeles

The Kris Munroe beach house is almost unrecognizable today. It now has a second level and the color has changed from red to gray. Looks like Kris must have gotten a substantial raise.

The Kris Munroe beach house is a private residence located in Pacific Cove, CA

The Santa Monica Pier is one of the best known locations used on Angels. It was the backdrop used in "The Sandcastle Murders" and "Angels in Waiting". Come down for a visit anytime and ride the carousel. And watch out for drugged Bosley staggering by.

The Carousel is open seven days a week. The Santa Monica Pier is located at 350 Santa Monica Pier, Santa Monica

Are you ready for a rub down? Jill and Bosley re-opened the Paradise Massage Parlor in "The Blue Angels". Look closely behind all those post-cards, and might just see Jill peak her head out.

The Paradise Massage Parlor is located at 54 Winword, Venice

Is that a photoplay? Marty's Combo is the hamburger/hot dog stand where Kelly learned what freeform films are all about in "Dirty Business". 30 years later, and Marty's is still open over business.

Marty's Combo is located at 10558 Pico Blvd, West Los Angeles

This is where we see the Angels walking side-by-side during the opening sequences for seasons 4 and 5. This same backdrop was slightly revised and used as the entrance into the Mother Goose Toy office in "Mother Goose is Running For His Life".

The office backdrop is located on the 20th Century Fox Studio Lot, Century City

Skating anyone? The Los Angeles Sports Arena was used in "Angels on Ice". Just watch out for Jo-Jo and Kelly popping wheelies in the park lot!

The Sports Arena is located at 3939 Figueroa Street, Los Angeles

The Ye Old Kings Head is the bar used in "Mother Goose is Running For His Life" in which Kelly sets up her cover as a "bug" expert. Inside the bar, there is a photo of Jaclyn and the crew taken as they were filming.

Ye Old Kings Head is located at 116 Santa Monica Blvd, Santa Monica

In the opening credits of every episode you see the Los Angeles Police Academy. The entrance still looks exactly the same day, except with one minor change - the Police Academy sign has been updated. Watch out for flying bullets from the shooting range.

The Police Academy is located at 1800 N Academy Dr, Los Angeles

Here is the Sabrina Duncan apartment building used in "Target Angels". Look closely at the window in the upper right hand corner, you just might see an exploding window and Jill screaming.

Sabrina Duncan's apartment building is located in Century City, Los Angeles

The Marina International Hotel was used inside and outside as a backdrop in "The Jade Trap". The outside looks virtually the same, while the inside has been updated and remodeled.

The Marina International Hotel is located in Marina Del Ray, Los Angeles

Lets go see Sally Storm's latest flick! In "Catch a Falling Angel", Tiffany and Kelly visit The Vista as it was the theatre that showcased Sally's work.

The Vista theatre is located at 4473 W Sunset Blvd, Los Angeles

And while you're in the area, you must stop and have a cup of coffee at "Guido's." Hopefully it won't be near as strong as Kelly's was in "Avenging Angels".

Guido's Restaurant is located at 11980 Santa Monica Blvd, Los Angeles

Farrah Fawcett

A Corpus Christi girl at heart, Farrah left her home town to attend The University of Texas, and began her major in Biology (later changed to Art). Farrah left college in her Junior year and headed to Hollywood. There she met Lee Majors and fell in love. One of Farrah's first films was **Myra Breckinridge** in 1969 and soon after she went on to be a semi-regular in Lee's series **Owen Marshall Attorney at Law** and **The Six Million Dollar Man**. Farrah and Lee married and she became known as "The Bionic Wife." Farrah's own career took a huge turn after she took a starring role in a new series called **Charlie's Angels.**

Farrah Fawcett-Majors became known as the sexy blond Jill Munroe. **Charlie's Angels** became a huge success and Farrah became a phenomenon. She was a house-hold name around the world, and before anyone knew it her famous "swimsuit pose" was hanging in everyone's bedroom. Farrah shocked the world when she left the hit series after only one year to pursue her film career. She went on to a court battle with the shows producers, Aaron Spelling and Leonard Goldberg. Farrah settled the court suit by appearing on **Charlie's Angels** for six episodes during the next two years. During that time, Farrah shot three films: **Somebody Killed Her Husband, Sunburn**, and **Saturn 3**.

Farrah and Lee split and she found her true love, Ryan O'Neal. Farrah returned to television in the film **Murder in Texas**, which she won the critics' praise. She was next found off Broadway performing the lead role in **Extremities**. Broadway critics raved about her performance which won her the title role in the television film, **The Burning Bed**. **The Burning Bed** was Farrah's strongest role of her long career.

After **The Burning Bed**, Farrah was never questioned as an actor again. Farrah went on to do the film version of **Extremities**. Soon after, Farrah was graced with her son, Redmond, by Ryan O'Neal. In 1991, Farrah and Ryan starred together in the short lived series **Good Sports**. In December of 1995 Farrah finally gave in and did a pictorial for **Playboy**. Farrah's **Playboy** issue sold over four million copies making it the biggest issue for **Playboy** for the nineties.

Most recently, Farrah shined in the Independent Film **The Apostle** which she received an nomination for Best Supporting Actress from **The Independent Spirit Awards**. Fawcett also released a best selling **Playboy** video titled "**All of Me**." In 1997, she split from her long time boyfriend Ryan O'Neal.

In 2003 Farrah brought her art center stage after she collaborated with artist, Keith Edmier with an art exhibition at the **Andy Warhol Museum** and a book titled, **Keith Edmier and Farrah Fawcett: Recasting Pygmalion**. Most recently, Fawcett starred in her own reality TV series **Chasing Farrah**. For more info checkout her website at www.farrahfawcett.us.

Series:
Owen Marshall Attorney at Law (semi-regular 1971-1974)
Harry O (semi-regular 1974-1976)
Charlie's Angels (1976-1977)
Good Sports (1991)
The Guardian (2002)
Spin City (2001)
Chasing Farrah (2005)

Plays
Butterflies are Free
Extremities

Specials:
Farrah Fawcett: All of Me (pay-for-view) 58 minutes
Farrah Fawcett: All of Me (video)70 minutes

Theatrical/ Television Films
The Apostle
Baby
Between Two Woman
Brave Little Toaster Goes To Mars
The Burning Bed
Cannonball Run
Children of the Dust
The Cookout
Criminal Behavior
Dalva
Double Exposure: The Margaret Bourke-White Story
Dr. T & The Women
Extremities
The Feminist and the Fuzz
The Flunky
Hollywood Wives: The New Generation
The Girl Who Came Gift Wrapped
The Great American Beauty Contest
Jewel
Logan's Run
The Lovemaster
Love is Funny Thing (UnHomme Qui Me Plait)
Man of the House
Murder In Texas
Murder on Flight 502
Myra Breckinridge
Natzi Hunter: The Beate Klarsfield Story
Poor Little Rich Girl
The Red Light Sting
Saturn 3
See You in the Morning
Small Sacrifices

Kate Jackson

After getting bitten by the acting bug, Kate moved from her home town of Birmingham, Alabama to New York City. While there, she enrolled in to the American Academy of Dramatic Arts. Kate's big break came when she played a "ghost" in the daytime drama, **Dark Shadows**. After three months on **Dark Shadows** she had guest roles on TV's **Bonanza** and a semi-regular on **NBC's** short-lived series, **The Jimmy Stewart Show**. She then hit the big time with a role on the crime show, **The Rookies**. Kate played nurse Jill Danko for producers Aaron Spelling and Leonard Goldberg. The producers decided after **The Rookies** ended that she was strong enough for her own series.

The producers and Kate created the skeleton shell for a series called **Charlie's Angels**. Kate was to become known around the world as the "smart" Angel. After a very successful three-year run, Kate decided to leave the series after the producers did not allow her out of her "Angel" contact to film **Kramer vs. Kramer.**

After **Charlie's Angels**, Kate tried her hand at comedy in the television remake of **Topper** (starring with first husband Andrew Stevens) and hit the big screen with the cutting edge film **Making Love**, about a man and his struggle with homosexuality. As her film career was blossoming, Kate was offered a new series for television called **Scarecrow and Mrs. King**. She fell in love with the character of Mrs. King (a mother of two boys who worked for a secret Government agency) and took on the series. Scarecrow became a huge hit. After four years, Scarecrow left the air. Kate returned to television the following year in **Baby Boom** which was based on the hit film.

The hardest role Kate had to play was her personal battle with breast cancer in 1987 and in 1989. She shared her experience with the world to show other women the importance of mammograms and cancer prevention.

In September 1995, Kate was given her greatest gift the adoption of her child, Charles Taylor Jackson. She has said being a mother is her greatest role. Kate has settled into motherhood and found herself in front of the camera in numerous projects. Kate is also a strong supporter of **RIF** (Reading Is Fundamental) and has lent her name to bring attention to this organization. Jackson continues to work in film and television.

Series:
Dark Shadows (1970-1971)
The Jimmy Stewart Show (1971-72)
The Rookies (1972-1976)
Charlie's Angels (1976-1979)
Scarecrow and Mrs. King (1983-1987)
Baby Boom (1988-1989)

Theatrical/Television films:
Adrift
Armed and Innocent
Cold Heart of a Killer
Cycling Through China
Death at Love House
Death Cruise
Death Scream
Dirty Tricks
Empty Cradle
Error in Judgment
Homewrecker
Inmates: A Love Story
Justice in a Small Town
A Kidnapping in the Family
Killer Bees
Larceny
Limbo
Listen to you Heart
Loverboy
Making Love
Miracle Dogs
A Mother's Testimony
The New Healers
Night of Dark Shadows
No Regrets
Panic in the Skies
Quiet Killer
Satan's School for Girls (1973)
Satan's School for Girls (2000)
Silence of Adultery
The Stranger Within
Sweet Deception
Thin Ice
Thunder and Lightning
What Happened to Bobby Earl?

Jaclyn Smith

Jaclyn Smith was born in Houston, Texas. Her ambition was to become a professional ballerina. She went to Trinity University in San Antonio and studied psychology and drama. After graduation she moved to New York to begin her modeling career.

Jaclyn quickly signed modeling contracts with **Max Factor** make-up and Breck hair products, and soon became known as the "Breck Girl."

After making a name in modeling Jaclyn moved to Los Angeles to begin her acting career. Her first film breaks were in **The Bootleggers** and **The Adventurers**. Jaclyn had guest appearances on **The Rookies**, **Switch**, and **McCloud.** In 1975, she auditioned for a new show called **Charlie's Angels** and won the role of Kelly Garrett. During the series run, Jaclyn fell in love for a second time to actor, Dennis Cole. But the whirl wind love affair ended in another divorce.

Although she was the only Angel to last all five years of the series, Jaclyn was already making a new name for herself as the "Queen of Miniseries.' After **Charlie's Angels** closed the office in 1981 and won critical and audience acclaim in such mini-series as **George Washington, Rage of Angels** and **Jacqueline Bouvier Kennedy.**

It was in 1980 while filming **Nightkill** with director Tony Richmond when Jaclyn fell in love once again. The couple married in 1981 and had two children, Gaston Anthony and Spencer Margaret. The marriage ended 8 years later.

In 1989, she returned to television with the short lived series, **Christine Cromwell.** Jaclyn continues working on her very successful **Kmart** signature line and her new furniture line.

In 1998 Jaclyn married for the 4th time to Dr. Bradley Allen. Jaclyn continues to work as an actress in television movies, but for this Angel her family comes first. Jaclyn, reprised her role of Kelly Garrett for the **Sony Pictures, Charlie's Angels: Full Throttle** in 2003. For more info on Jaclyn go to www.jaclynsmith.com.

Series:
Switch (1975-1976)
Charlie's Angels (1976-1981)
Christine Cromwell (1989-1990)
The District (2002)

Theatrical/Television Films
Adventurers
Before He Wakes
The Bootleggers (a.k.a Bootlegger's Angels)
The Bourne Identity
Charlie's Angels: Full Throttle
Cries Unheard: The Donna Yaklich Story
Deja Vu
Escape from Bogen County
Family Album
Florence Nightingale
Freefall
George Washington
Goodbye Columbus
In the Arms of a Killer
Jacqueline Bouvier Kennedy
Kaleidoscope
Lies Before Kisses
Love Can Be Murder
Married to a Stranger
My Very Best Friend
Navigating the Heart
Nightkill
Nightmare in the Daylight
The Night They Saved Christmas
Ordinary Miracles
Probe
Rage of Angels
Rage of Angels II: The Story Continues
The Rape of Dr. Willis
Sentimental Journey
Settle the Score
Three Secerts
The Users
The Whiz Kid and the Carnival Caper
Windmills of the Gods

Series:
Search (semi regular 1972-1973)
Josie and the Pussycats (1970-1972)
Charlie's Angels (1977-1981)
One West Waikiki (CBS 1994 Syndicated: 1995-1996)
Las Vegas (2000-present)

Specials:
The Cheryl Ladd Special
Cheryl Ladd: Scenes from a Special
Cheryl Ladd: Fascinated
Cheryl Ladd: Souvenirs

Plays:
Annie Get Your Gun

Theatrical/Television Films
Bluegrass
Broken Promises: Taking Emily Back
Changes
Crash: The Mystery of Flight 1501
Crossings
Dancing with Danger
Dead Before Dawn
Deadly Care
A Death in California
A Dog of Flanders
Eve's Christmas
Every Mothers Worst Fear
Evil in the Deep
The Fulfillment of Mary Gray
The Girl Who Came Between Them
The Grace Kelly Story
The Hasty Heart
The Haunting of Lisa
Though None Go With Me
Her Best Friends Husband
Jekyll & Hyde
Kentucky Woman
Kiss & Tell
Lisa
Locked Up: A Mother's Rage
Marriage of a Young Stockbroker
Michael Landon, The Father I Knew
Millennium
Now and Forever
Perfect Little Angels
Permanent Midnight
Poison Ivy
Purple Hearts
Romance on the Orient Express
Satan's School for Girls
Though None Go With Me
Treasure of Jamaica Reef
A Tangled Web
When She Was Bad

Cheryl Ladd

Cheryl Ladd grew up in South Dakota as Cheryl Stoppelmoor. She sang in a band called **The Music Shop Band** during high school. After Cheryl graduated she and the band went on tour. The band found themselves in Los Angeles and eventually broke up. Cheryl stayed in LA to pursue her dream as an actress. Cheryl's big professional break was singing back-up on the cartoon series **Josie and the Pussycats**. It was while filming **Jamaica Reef** in 1973 she met her first husband David Ladd, son of the famous actor Alan "Laddie" Ladd. 1974, Cheryl, gave birth to their daughter, Jordan.

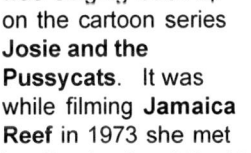

In 1976, Cheryl lost the role of Nancy in the series **Family** to Meredith Baxter Birney. The producers of Family had another hit TV show called **Charlie's Angels** in which they were looking for a new Angel. Aaron Spelling and Leonard Goldberg asked Cheryl if she would take the job. After Cheryl turned down the series twice, she finally accepted the role of Jill Munroe's little sister, Kris in 1977. She captured the hearts of America and kept the series alive.

During the series, Cheryl was able to record two albums, **Cheryl Ladd** (1978) and **Dance Forever** (1979). She had a top 40 hit "Think It Over" and was also a #1 recording artist in Japan. She also released a third album **Take a Chance** (1980), it was only released in Japan. During **Charlie's Angels**, Cheryl's marriage to David Ladd ended and she fell in love and married, Brian Russell.

Cheryl moved on, working in many successful television films such as **The Grace Kelly Story, Bluegrass** and **Changes**. In 1993, Cheryl appeared in the cult classic film **Poison Ivy** and in 1994 found herself returning to TV in a new series, **One West Waikiki**.

In 1996, Cheryl opened another creative door with writing a children's book with husband Brian Russell, **The Adventures of Little Nettie Windship**. Cheryl was also the first Angel to have her very own website to stay in touch with her fans at www.cherylladd.com

Cheryl donates her time as a Goodwill Ambassador for CHILDHELP USA and can be seen weekly on the hit **NBC** series **Las Vegas**.

She recently released the book **Token Chick: A Woman's Guide To Golfing With The Boys**, an autobiographical book recounting her experiences with the sport of golf.

Shelley Hack

Shelley Hack began her career of modeling in the mid-sixties while still in her early teens. Shelley made a big name for herself in the print ad industry. She branched out into acting in the mid-seventies with Woody Allen's **Annie Hall** and **If I Ever See You Again**. These films helped her land the lead in the television film, **Death Car on the Freeway.**

By the late seventies, Shelley was tagged as the "Charlie Girl" while promoting **Revlon's** No. 1 "Charlie" cologne in print ads. The "Charlie" cologne ads brought Shelley to the attention of Aaron Spelling and Leonard Goldberg. The **Charlie's Angels** producers had to replace actress Kate Jackson and decided to hire Shelley Hack because of her classic looks.

Although Shelley's character Tiffany Welles was let go at the end of her first year, Shelley moved on and starred in other series, **Cutter to Houston** and **Jack & Mike**. Shelley has done a large body of acting work, which included stage, theatrical films and television appearances.

In the 1990's, Shelley ran for a government office; however she was not elected.

She lives in Los Angeles with her husband and daughter. Currently Hack works in media development in post conflict and developing economies with her firm **Shelley Hack Media Consulting.**

Series
Charlie's Angels (1979-1980)
Cutter to Houston (1983)
Jack and Mike (1985-1986)

Theatrical/Television Films
Annie Hall
Blind Fear
Bridesmaids
A Casualty of War
Close Ties
Death Car on the Freeway
Falling from the Sky-Flight 174
The Finishing Touch
Frequent Flyer
House Arrest
If Ever I See You Again
Kicks
King of Comedy
Me, Myself and I
My Secret Angel
Not in my Family
Perry Mason: The Case of the Wicked Wives
Single Bars, Single Women
The Stepfather
Taking Back My Life: The Nancy Ziegenmeyer Story
Seaquest DSV
Time After Time
Trackdown: Finding the Goodbar Killer
Troll
Vanities

Tanya Roberts

Tanya started her career working in modeling, working in commercials and acting in off-Broadway plays. In 1977, she moved to LA with husband Barry Roberts to give her career a boost. She worked on several films and was even signed to the rival Angel show called **Flying High**; however she was dropped from the cast when it was being retooled.

Aaron Spelling and Leonard Goldberg hired Tanya for a spin off of their hit series **Vega$**, called **Ladies in Blue. Ladies in Blue** never became a series but did put Tanya in the minds of the producers. Spelling and Goldberg were searching to find the hottest actresses to give their show **Charlie's Angels** new life. Tanya beat out 2000 young hopefuls for the role of Julie Rogers in the series. The series came to an end after her first season in 1981.

Series
That 70's Show (1998-2001)
Charlie's Angels (1980-1981)
Hotline (1996)

Theatrical/Television Films
Almost Pregnant
The Beastmaster
Body Slam
California Dreaming
Deep Down
Fingers
Forced Entry
Hearts and Armor
Inner Sanctum
Jacob's Challenge
Legal Tender
Murder Me, Murder You
National Lampoon's Favorite Deadly Sins
Night Eyes
Pleasure Cove
The Private Files of J. Edgar Hoover
Purgatory
Racquet
Sheena
Sins of Desire
Tourist Trap
Twisted Justice
A View to a Kill
Waikiki
Yum Yum Girls
Zuma Beach

Tanya's career got a great boost from the Angels. She went on to star in three major feature films: **The Beastmaster, Sheena: Queen of the Jungle** and James Bond's **A View to a Kill.** Tanya then went on to star in the CD-ROM called **The Pandora Directive** and in the **Cinemax's** series **Hotline**.

In 1998, Tanya co-starred in the hit **FOX** series, **That 70's Show** for three seasons. Tanya continues to peruse her acting career. Most recently on the **Showtime** series, **Barbershop**. She still lives in Los Angels.

Tanya's husband Barry Roberts passed away in 2006, the twosome had been married for 32 years.

David Doyle

David Doyle grew up in Nebraska in a tight loving family. He spent two years at The University of Nebraska studying Latin. In 1950, he began attending New York's Neighborhood Playhouse where he began working on his acting career. His first big break was when he replaced Walter Matthau on Broadway in the show **Will Success Spoil Rock Hunter?**. David moved on to work in numerous productions and directing over 60 plays. It was not until David hit Hollywood that he became a notable face. His first feature film break was starring with Kris Kristofferson in Vigilante Force. David then worked on a couple of TV series. He played the Irish dad in Bridget Loves Bernie and the star's boss in **The New Dick Van Dyke Show.**

After Doyle's first wife Rachel died, he vowed never to marry again; however he was swept off his feet by an actress named Anne Nathan when the two worked on a revival of **South Pacific**. The happy couple found Anne was stricken with the hereditary eye disease, Retinitis Pigmentosa. David worked throughout his life to educate others on Retinitis Pigmentosa.

It was in 1976 when David signed on to the role of Bosley for a pilot film by Aaron Spelling and Leonard Goldberg called **Charlie's Angels**. Although his part was small in the pilot, when **ABC** picked Angels up for the fall season, Aaron and Leonard combined the lawyer and Bosley characters together and David Doyle became Charlie's only male Angel. David stayed with the series throughout its full run (1976-1981).

During the 80's, Doyle worked on many pilot's for series and did many stage and film productions. In the 90's, Doyle worked on the successful children's series **Rugrats** as the voice of Grandpa Pickles and the voice of Pepe of the major motion picture **The Adventures of Pinocchio**. David Doyle died on February 26, 1997, of a heart attack. David has one daughter, Leah, from his first marriage.

Series
- Rugrats
- General Hospital
- Charlie's Angels
- Bridget Loves Bernie

Theatrical/Television Films
- Love or Money
- Pursuit of Happiness
- No way to Treat a Lady
- Paper Lion
- Who Killed Mary What's her Name
- Tiger Makes out
- A New Leaf
- The April Fools
- Loving
- Act One
- Vigilante Force
- Capricorn One
- Coogan's Bluff
- Happy Anniversary Waltz
- Making It
- The Come Back
- Lady Liberty
- Blood Sport
- Black Market Babies
- Archie (pilot)
- Sooner or Later
- Maybe Baby
- The Invisible Woman
- Wait till your Mother gets Home
- Ghost Writer
- The Blue and Gray

Theatre-Broadway
- The Beauty Part
- Here's Love
- I was Dancing
- Something About a Soldier
- South Pacific
- Will Success Spoil Rock Hunter

Memories of David Doyle

"David was a wonderful human being and a joy to be around. He was a man who worked tirelessly in the fight against Retinitis Pigmentosa. I love the twinkle in his eye, the gravel in his voice, the joy in his quick witted laughter. David will always have a place in my heart."
- Kate Jackson

"He was one of the kindest, gentlest people on the planet. I will miss him terribly." - Cheryl Ladd

"David was one of the nicest people I ever worked with in my life. A man filled with humor, love and sincerity. I will miss him."
-Aaron Spelling

"David Doyle always brought a smile to my face and made me laugh. My heart goes out to his family. My memories will always be treasured of a dear sweet friend." - Jaclyn Smith

David Doyle passed away on February 26, 1997, at the age of 67. His career consisted of over fifty films, Broadway shows, many television series including **Bridget Loves Bernie, The New Dick Van Dyke Show,** and **Nickelodeon's Rugrats** as the voice of Grandpa Pickles. Doyle also had guest appearances on **Aaron Spelling's Sunset Beach, ABC's Lois and Clark** and **New Line Cinema's The Adventures of Pinocchio.**

But how can you forget the lovable "Bosley, John Bosley", who was the cornerstone for the Angels throughout the series entire run (1976-1981). "Charlie should be calling right…now!" or his unforgettable wonderful warm laughter that rang throughout his life and career. David Doyle will be greatly missed by his loved ones, the Angels, and by millions of people around the world. *We Miss You David!!!*

John Forsythe

John Forsythe grew up in New Jersey after he attended the University of North Carolina, he moved to New York City for his true passion, acting. John received his stage training at the well known New York's Actors Studio.

In 1944, John made his motion picture debut in "Destinations Tokyo." On Broadway, John worked in such powerhouse plays as "Teahouse of the August Moon" and "All my Sons."

It was not until 1957 that John took the role of Bentley Gregg in the hit television series, **Bachelor Father** which made him a star. The series ran for six years. After the cancellation he went on to work in two more series, **The John Forsythe Show** (1965) and **To Rome with Love** (1969).

In 1975 Forsythe got a phone call from his buddy Aaron Spelling asking him to record the voice of a detective agency ownee Charles Townsend for the new Spelling/Goldberg TV movie **Charlie's Angels**. Forsythe continued as the voice of Charlie until the series ended in 1981. After **Charlie's Angels** ended, he moved into the mansion on **Dynasty**, another television hit by producers Aaron Spelling and Douglas Cramer. The series aired from 1981 - 1989.

Forsythe has continued to work in television with guest appearances. In 1993 he worked on a new series **I Witnessed Video**.

Forsythe came back to the speaker box as Charles Townsend for the Sony theatrical movies **Charlie's Angels** (2000) & **Charlie's Angels: Full Throttle** (2003).

Series
- Bachelor Father (1957-1962)
- The John Forsythe Show (1965-1966)
- To Rome with Love (1969 - 1971)
- The World of Survival (1971-77) narrative
- Charlie's Angels (1976-1981) uncredited
- Dyansty (1981-1989)
- I Wittness Video (1981)

Theatrical/Television Films
- Charlie's Angels: Full Throttle (2003)
- Charlie's Angels (2000)
- Hotel de Love (1997)
- Scrooged (1988)
- On Fire (1987)
- Mysterious Two (1982)
- Follow Me if You Dare (1982)
- Sizzle (1981)
- Time for Miracles (1980)
- ...And Justice for All (1979)
- Cruise Into Terror (1978)
- The Users (1978/ABC)
- With This Ring (1978)
- Never Con a Killer (1977)
- Tail Gunner Joe (1977)
- The Deadly Tower (1976)
- Amelia Earhart (1976)
- Terror on the 40th Floor (1974)
- The Healers (1974)
- Cry Panic (1974)
- Lisa, Bright and Dark (1973)
- The Letters (1973)
- Topaz (1969)
- The Happy Ending (1969)
- Shadow on the Land (1968)
- In Cold Blood (1967)
- Madame X (1966)
- Sweet Taste of Vengeance (1966)
- Kitten With a Whip (1964)
- See How they Run (1964)
- The Ambassador's Daughter (1956)
- Everything but The Truth (1956)
- The Trouble With Harry (1055)
- The Glass Web (1953)
- Escape From Fort Bravo (1953)
- It Happens Every Thursday (1953)
- Westinghouse Studio One - "Pagoda" (1952)
- The Captive City (1952)
- Westinghouse Studio One - "Hold Back the Night" (1952)
- Westinghouse Studio One - "No Tears for Hilda" (1951)
- Westinghouse Studio One - "None but My Foe" (1951)
- Northern Pursuit (1943)
- Destination Tokyo (1943)

Forsythe has been married three times, first a very brief marriage to Parker McCormick; then to Julie Warren. He has three daughters, Dall, Page and Brooke. One highlight in Forsythe's life was being the "Voice of the Dodgers" for two innings when Red Barber took a small break.

Aaron Spelling

Aaron Spelling grew up the son of a poor Jewish immigrants in Dallas, Texas. He attended Southern Methodist University where he won the prestigious Harvard Award for best original one-act play and was the only student to direct a major play in the history of SMU. After graduation Spelling moved to Hollywood in 1953. As an actor, Spelling appeared in more than fifty shows and a dozen films. He appeared in **Dragnet, Gunsmoke** and **I Love Lucy**. In 1954, Spelling began his writing career with the **Zane Grey** series, **Last Man** and **Playhouse 90**. Four years later Spelling produced his first series called **Johnny Ringo**. He went on to be producer for two other series. Spelling started his first partnership with Danny Thomas. During the three year partnership they produced **The Danny Thomas Show, The Guns of Will Sonne, The Mod Squad**, plus six movies of the week for **ABC-TV**.

Angel Thoughts

""Aaron's contributions in television are unequaled. To me he was a dear friend and a truly genuine human being."
~ Jaclyn Smith

"We have lost a giant of the television industry, Aaron Spelling. I will be eternally grateful for the opportunity he provided me and my sympathies are with his family. He will be sorely missed."
~ Cheryl Ladd

In 1971, Spelling formed a partnership with Leonard Goldberg and produced 38 television films and many top rated series including **Charlie's Angels, Starsky and Hutch, Fantasy Island, Hart to Hart** and **Family**. During the late 80's, Spelling's company moved into theatrical films by producing such hits as, **Mr. Mom, 'night Mother** and **Soapdish**. Spelling also has produced some of the most talked about television movies in history of television with **The Boy in the Plastic Bubble, Day One, And The Band Played On**. Spelling won Emmy's for **Day One & And The Band Played On**.

A new generation got to know Spelling during the 90s with his mega TV hits, **Beverly Hills 90210, Melrose Place, 7th Heaven** and **Charmed**.

Aaron Spelling has been married twice. His first marriage was to actress, Carolyn Jones (**The Addams Family**). The couple divorced before their careers were successful! A few years later, Spelling met Candy Marer. He fell in love and has been married ever since. Candy and Aaron have two children, Tori and Randy. Candy is seen on **QVC** selling her dolls with profits going to Centro de Ninos, a free daycare for the poor. Tori played Donna on **Beverly Hills, 90210** and most recently her **VH1** series, **So Notorious**. Randy worked on the day time drama, **Sunset Beach**.

TVs fell silent on June 23, 2006 when Aaron Spelling passed away. He was 83.

Leonard Goldberg

Leonard Goldberg has long been considered one of the entertainment industry's most talented, successful and creative executives and producers. In 2000 & 2003 he produced both feature films based on **Charlie's Angels** at his production company, **Mandy Films, Inc.** He co-partners with his daughter Amanda Goldberg, who was the associate producer of both films.

Goldberg has served as Head of Programming for a major network (**ABC**) and President of a major Hollywood studio (**Twentieth Century-Fox**). At **ABC**, he was responsible for developing and introducing an entirely new format the Made-For-Television Movie. As a television producer he was responsible for some of the most highly acclaimed telefilms ever made, including **Brian's Song, The Boy in the Plastic Bubble, Something About Amelia** and **Alex: The Life of a Child**.

In partnership with Aaron Spelling he was responsible for an unprecedented string of hit television series, including **Charlie's Angels, Hart to Hart, The Rookies, Starsky & Hutch, Fantasy Island** and **Family**. Under his own banner, he produced the spectacularly successful features **WarGames** and **Sleeping With The Enemy** and the Eddie Murphy comedy **Distinguished Gentleman**. During his time as President of **Twentieth Century-Fox**, the studio produced such critically acclaimed hit films as **Broadcast News, Big, Die Hard, Wall Street**, and **Working Girl**.

After being in the entertainment business for over 40 years, Goldberg still has the magic touch!

Mike Pingel

Mike Pingel; actor, writer, publicist and creator of the first ever **Charlie's Angels** newsletter in 1995 called **Angelic Heaven**. He went on to open the number one fan site for **Charlie's Angels** fans at www.charliesangels.com. The site has been Keeping fans up-to-date with the actresses & the series since 1996 (which means the site has lasted longer than the original series!) The website receives over 5,400+ visitors daily. **CharliesAngels.com** was the picked "Site of the Day" by **Yahoo!** and **Web TV** in 1996.

Pingel's collection is very sought after too! His "Charlie's Angels" lunchbox co-starred with Jennie Garth & Jason Priestley on Aaron Spelling's series, **Beverly Hills 90210**. His collection has also been used for the 1997 **Columbia-TRI Star Home Video Charlie's Angels** video releases in 1997, the 2006 DVD release of **Charlie's Angels: The Complete Third Season,** and was seen on the **Charlie's Angels: The Complete First Season** DVD.

In 2000, Pingel was brought into "consultation" with Drew Barrymore, Leonard Goldberg, Amanda Goldberg and director McG. Pingel helped layout the floor plan for the office (which is the featured in this book.) He even auditioned for the role of Cameron Diaz's boyfriend, but was never used in the movie.

Pingel & his collection have been featured on many shows including: **Entertainment Tonight, Dateline NBC, E! Entertainment, TV Land, The Learning Channel, Inside Edition, A&E, Good Day LA, Deco Drive, The Arthel and Fred Show , The Drum (New Zealand), K-ABC, K-CBS, The BBC Radio , Retro 70's Show, (Canadian) USA Today, Yahoo!, Who Weekly, TVGuide.com, Los Angeles Magazine, The Net, Edge, English Express, New Zealand Weekly** and **Sony's Charlie's Angels: The Complete First Season DVD.** He has also helped numerous productions produce segments including **Dateline NBC "All of Her", Dick Clark "All Star Party for Aaron Spelling", "Entertainment Tonight: 20th Anniversary of Charlie's Angels"** and with **Late Night with David Letterman, Spelling Entertainment,** and **Columbia Home Video.**

Pingel did his undergraduate work at The American University in Washington , D.C. where he received his BA in Theater. He has worked in front of the camera in such memorable shows as **America's Most Wanted** and **Dream West**. Most recently, he was seen in Marc Anthony's video "Ahora Quien" and Farrah Fawcett's **Chasing Farrah.** He can be heard weekly every Wednesday on the radio on **Daytona & Friends** doing **The Hollywood Minute.**

In 2006, Pingel had an exhibit of his **Charlie's Angels** collection for the public at the **Hollywood Entertainment Museum**. The exhibit ran from May 18, 2006 - June 30, 2006. On display were the **Charlie's Angels** dolls, dresses, lunchbox, dress up set, etc. Over 60 items were showcased.

For updates on Mike Pingel go to www.mikepingel.com or www.charliesangels.com.